ISSUES IN
JUVENILE DELINQUENCY

American Correctional Association Monographs
Number 10

American Correctional Association
4321 Hartwick Road, Suite L-208
College Park, Maryland 20740
(301) 699-7600

Other monographs in this series

Women in Corrections
Correctional Management
Jails
Classification
Community Corrections
The Status of Probation and Parole?
Corrections and Public Awareness
Issues in Juvenile Corrections
Correctional Officers: Power, Pressure and Responsibility

Also of related interest

Prisons and Kids

Publication Staff: Linda Dziobek, Darlene Megahan, Rick Neimiller, Editorial Staff; Martin Pociask, Illustrations; Alonzo Winfield, Layout; Lisa Hanson, Annette Ryburn, Typesetters.

Cover illustration by Martin Pociask

CONTENTS

PREFACE

With the publication of *Issues in Juvenile Delinquency*, its latest monograph, the American Correctional Association continues its tradition of offering thought-provoking, stimulating, and relevant discussions on topics that are of specific concern within corrections.

ACA monographs are tailored to the information needs of line staff, administrators, practitioners, and/or students of corrections. The overall purpose is to provide pertinent and timely information to our members and others who are interested in varied corrections issues. The Association is confident that the many monographs produced in the coming years will encourage the exchange of information and ideas that is crucial to progressive change both within and without the field.

Issues in Juvenile Delinquency covers the spectrum of delinquency issues. It includes classification of and advocacy for juveniles, training of juvenile personnel, prevention programs, and the care and treatment of "mentally disordered" and violent juveniles, as well as an overview of teen court. The monograph offers practical advice to facility managers and treatment staff working in the juvenile field, providing empirical support for conclusions reached and suggestions made. Contributors could compose a who's who list of professionals in corrections—each one uniquely suited to discuss the topic at hand and representing a different branch of the corrections family.

Issues in Juvenile Delinquency also showcases the significant issues being raised in juvenile corrections at a time when juvenile offenders are being incarcerated at an ever increasing rate. It is the goal of the Association that, through these pages, readers will gain insight into the problems that practitioners face and the solutions that are possible.

The ACA takes a considerable interest in juvenile corrections and has contributed to its improvement by devising a National Correctional Policy on Juvenile Corrections, ratified by ACA's Delegate Assembly on August 23, 1984. One of 21 national correctional policies passed by the Association since late 1983, ACA's juvenile corrections policy recommends positive changes in the field involving communications, quality programming, family/community involvement, deinstitutionalization of status offenders, and more. It is hoped that *Issues in Juvenile Delinquency* will contribute still further to the process of enhancing this critical area within corrections.

Anthony P. Travisono
Executive Director
American Correctional Association

INTRODUCTION

Juvenile justice is an area of the justice system that has fostered a number of major philosophical debates in recent years. It is a system that developed as an outgrowth of the emergence of new knowledge in education and social sciences during the first half of the century. While its antecedents have ancient historical beginnings, since 1900 it is the system known as juvenile justice that has espoused hope for wayward youth and has enunciated a protective, caring, and parental role for the state as it administers juvenile programs. The cornerstone of the system has been the doctrine of *in loco parentis* or the belief that the state has a legitimate obligation to function as a parent—in the place of the parent—when it intervenes in the life of a juvenile and removes a juvenile from parental control. This basic premise persists and is evident in the statutes of most state juvenile codes.

For juvenile corrections the justice system has meant the development and operation of programs designed to treat youth on an individual basis and provide the necessary custody and care that promote their development into productive adult citizens. The punishment and "just deserts" doctrine, in vogue for adult corrections, is not an operational goal for juvenile justice. Punishment, if it exists, is part of a structured educational process that stimulates behavioral control and nurtures appropriate growth processes.

Despite recent controversy about the mission of juvenile justice, this collection of quality articles exemplifies several interesting perspectives in a number of specific areas. Jeanne Cyriaque presents a sophisticated identification scheme that may be of assistance to agencies currently coping with serious offenders. Her article "Who is the Serious Juvenile Offender?" utilizes a wealth of accumulated computerized data in a large midwestern state. Daniel Maloney reviews training perspectives for staff involved with serious offenders in an article titled "Working with Troubled Youths: Considerations for the New Professional." His approach is common sense and encompasses a proven training perspective. "Handling Violent Juveniles" by Edward Murphy details the Massachusetts effort to cope with the violent juvenile. Mr. Murphy's approach catalogs one agency's efforts to unite the treatment mission with the need to effect custodial controls.

Unique approaches with a broad appeal characterize articles by S. Christopher Baird, "Classifying Juveniles: An Important Management Tool"; Melvin Brown, "Training Officers in Juvenile Detention"; M. Amos Clifford, "Turning Point Youth Services: A Delinquency Prevention Project"; Richard Everitt, "Tracking Children Within a Regional Delinquency Prevention System"; Natalie Rothstein, "Teen Court: Involving Young People in the Judicial Process"; and Joseph Sweet, "Probation as Therapy." Each of these articles discusses an ongoing operational program that can be observed by interested persons.

The Eliot Hartstone article "Turnstile Children: Falling Between the Cracks" is an excellent presentation of the ever-growing problems for correctional agencies who attempt to program mentally disordered offenders. Mr. Hartstone offers practical definitions and a listing of well-organized programs that serve as an excellent information source.

Allen Breed's article "Juvenile Justice: A Challenge for Change" is a detailed discussion of juvenile justice philosophy and practice. Mr. Breed, in effective and certain language, discusses the turmoil created by conflicting ideologies in juvenile justice. His special emphasis on the "mission" of juvenile corrections offers guidelines for those with an interest in the field.

Thus, *Issues in Juvenile Delinquency* is excellent reading for the scholar and the practitioner and supplies thoughtful and relevant information to all concerned.

Samuel Sublett Jr.
Illinois Department of Corrections

Classifying Juveniles:
An Important Management Tool

S. Christopher Baird

---

*As corrections turns away from the medical
model of rehabilitation, expectations of
classification have changed dramatically.
It is now viewed as a major management
tool for corrections.*

The dominant correctional philosophy applied today is punishment/control rather than treatment/rehabilitation for adult offenders and, increasingly, for juvenile offenders. However, increased emphasis on control will not be effective if uniformly applied to all youths. Juveniles differ considerably in terms of type of offense, likelihood of recommitting crimes, emotional needs, education levels, vocational skills, honesty, and other factors. To deal effectively with this variety of people and problems requires an understanding of the individual as well as knowledge and flexibility in applying different supervision techniques.

Because not all juvenile offenders require the same level of supervision or exhibit the same problems, most experienced probation and aftercare officers use an intuitive system of classifying offenders into different treatment and surveillance modes. Thus, classification decisions usually are based on judgments of clients' needs and officers' perceptions of their clients' potential for continued unlawful behavior. It seems reasonable to assume that without this type of case load management successes would diminish and failures would increase. However, this untested, highly individualized approach does not provide the information necessary to deploy staff and other resources rationally. Criteria used to determine the appropriate supervision level are probably as varied as officers' experiences, educations, and philosophical approaches to the job.

In 1983 and 1984, consultants from Isthmus Associates, Inc., head-quartered in Madison, Wisconsin, drafted a series of technical assistance reports to help correctional agencies in six states develop and implement juvenile classification systems. The Office of Juvenile Justice and Delinquency Prevention (OJJDP) funded this effort. The agencies were located in Orange County and Contra Costa, California, and in Hennepin County, Minnesota, as well as in Louisiana, New Mexico, Hawaii, and Wisconsin. To devise appropriate classification systems, consultants spent several days interviewing agency staff in each community about operational problems and directions those operations might take. From this research and other explorations, elements of a model classification system emerged.

Disappointing Results

Classification systems are designed to bring structure and consisten-cy to correctional decision making. Yet the history of juvenile classification is littered with disappointing results. Many past attempts at classification were based on treatment models. The I-Level System, developed initially for use in the California Department of the Youth Authority, is perhaps the best known clinically based typology system. This system classifies youths into groups such as "manipula-tors" and "cultural conformists" for which specific counseling strategies have been developed. Initially, I-Level classifications were based on data obtained during an interview, but the same basic classifications can be derived through use of a multiple-choice ques-tionnaire (the Jesness Inventory).

As corrections turns away from the medical model of rehabilitation, expectations of classification have changed dramatically. Classifica-tion is now viewed as a major management tool for corrections and a means for enhancing consistency and equity in decision making. The major classification effort of the last decade, the National Institute of Corrections' (NIC) Model Classification Project, combines elements of control and casework into a comprehensive program incorporating the following elements:

- Classification based on risk of continued criminal activity and the offender's need for services

- Case management classification system designed to help probation and parole officers develop effective case plans and select appropriate casework strategies
- Management information system designed to enhance planning, monitoring, evaluation, and accountability
- Work load deployment system allowing agencies to allocate their limited resources effectively and efficiently

This system, currently used by hundreds of agencies throughout the United States and Canada, has become the dominant model of offender classification in adult probation and parole. Advocates of the system have lobbied hard for development of a parallel process for managing juvenile probation and aftercare.

Model Risk Instrument

Risk assessment, an element of a classification system, traditionally means the process of determining the probability an individual will repeat unlawful or destructive behavior. Risk prediction can take several forms such as predicting violent behavior, any new offense (recidivism), or technical violation of probation or parole. Each type of behavior represents a different degree of concern for the correctional system and the community in general. For example, while past research indicates property offenders are the group most likely to recidivate, it is violent offenders who represent a greater physical danger and inspire greater fear in the community. To be of maximum value to decision makers, risk assessment must consider all these concerns along with moral and legal issues surrounding each one.

Consultants sponsored by OJJDP set out to determine what risk assessment variables should be used to establish supervision levels for juveniles. They obtained risk instruments from several jurisdictions and compared items from these scales with those identified through past research efforts. Finally, the consultants obtained new data from the six correctional agencies with whom they worked to develop and implement juvenile classification systems.

The review of various risk instruments currently being used indicated the scales had a considerable number of items in common. Each risk scale reviewed used ratings of substance abuse, prior criminal involvement, and emotional stability. Some of the scales were obviously adapted from adult risk assessment instruments and contained variables of questionable validity when applied to juveniles; others were based on an analysis of juvenile characteristics related to probation/aftercare success or failure. The latter group tended to use additional risk indices such as school problems, presence of learning disabilities, and family problems. Most reviewed scales contained a measure of client attitude that was clearly adopted from risk instruments used in adult probation.

Use of the scales was generally too new to have generated much data regarding their accuracy. In other instances, follow-up data were not collected systematically after scales were implemented. Thus, additional validity measures were not available.

While most early research efforts in juvenile risk prediction dealt exclusively with parole (aftercare), results did present some guidelines for probation risk scale development. Studies conducted in Illinois (Baird 1974), California (Wenk 1975; Wenk and Emerick 1976), and Wisconsin (Baird and Heinz 1978) indicated prior criminal involvement indices such as age at first adjudication, number of prior adjudications, and number of prior commitments were the best available predictors of future behavior. These studies also noted institutional adjustment (Illinois), drug usage (California), and emotional stability (Wisconsin) increased the overall predictiveness of each statistical equation.

To further augment development of a generic risk instrument, data were obtained from the six correctional agencies. The data varied in quality and quantity among sites as did the point of correctional intervention from which data were obtained (probation or correctional facility placement). These differences prevented merging the information into a single data file. Despite this drawback, separate analysis of each data set proved valuable to the construction of a model risk instrument.

Based on all the information reviewed, the following elements seem universally predictive of continued criminal involvement for juveniles:

- Age at first adjudication
- Prior criminal behavior (a combined measure of the number and severity of priors)
- Number of prior commitments to juvenile facilities

- Drug/chemical abuse
- Alcohol abuse
- Family relationships (parental control)
- School problems
- Peer relationships

Assessing Program Needs

Needs assessments in juvenile corrections should be an integral part of a classification system. By including needs assessments in the classification process, an agency not only addresses custody requirements and community protection issues, but also the rehabilitative needs of juveniles. While most probation and aftercare workers deal with the program needs of youth, a structured, formalized needs assessment component:

- Ensures that certain types of problems are considered and helps to formulate a case plan
- Provides an additional measure for setting priorities (i.e., judging the amount of effort that should be expended on an individual case relative to the entire case load)
- Provides a base for monitoring a juvenile's progress
- Forces qualitative review of every case through periodic reassessments and provides a basis for judging the relative effectiveness of the case plan and casework approach leading to changes where appropriate
- Provides a data base for coherent planning and evaluation of programs, policies, and procedures

The consultants for OJJDP's classification study reviewed juvenile needs assessment instruments constructed in California, Illinois, Montana, and Wisconsin. They found such commonly used need items as vocational skills, alcohol abuse, health, and family finances. Need scales used in juvenile corrections are quite similar in content and format. All agencies involved in developing a classification system should be guided by the maxim "simple is better." Complex systems are difficult to complete and reliability often is less than desirable.

The planning and evaluation potential provided by a formal needs assessment system should not be overlooked. In an era of limited resources, agencies must strive to obtain the best results from each dollar spent. Assessments of needs, periodically completed on each ward, can be used to measure progress, evaluate the relative effectiveness of programs, and plan future projects.

Reclassification and Supervision

In the view of most staffs interviewed, reclassification should occur relatively frequently because the situations of juvenile clients change rapidly. Further, risk assessment at reclassification should emphasize adjustment rather than predictive factors. Data collected in one study site indicated that, while subjective judgments of probation officers made at intake demonstrated little correlation with success or failure, the same judgment made after 90 or more days' experience with a youth had considerable validity. The role of reclassification is to structure these ratings by requiring that all staff consider the same criteria in establishing supervision levels.

In changing emphasis from criminal history and other factors noted at intake to factors describing adjustment to supervision at reassessment, youths can be moved to lower or higher supervision levels based on actual behavior. The system thus assumes a "just deserts" approach to setting supervision levels.

In probation and aftercare, supervision standards delineate the minimum number and type of required contacts at each supervision level, thereby incorporating a level of accountability into a system where performance is inherently difficult to quantify. The one drawback of establishing minimum contact standards is that, over time, minimum requirements may become the operational norm. It is therefore extremely important to incorporate a casework audit procedure into the system to ensure contacts respond to the needs and risk of each case, exceeding minimum standards where appropriate. Examples of standards used in probation and aftercare are presented below:

Regular Supervision
- Four face-to-face contacts per month with youth
- Two face-to-face contacts per month with parents

- One face-to-face contact per month with placement staff
- One contact with school officials

Intensive Supervision
- Six face-to-face contacts per month with youth
- Three face-to-face contacts per month with parents
- One face-to-face contact per month with placement staff
- Two contacts with school officials

Alternative Care Cases
- One face-to-face contact per month with youth
- Four contacts with agency staff with one to be face-to-face
- One contact every two months with parents

Assignments to supervision levels are usually based on both risk and needs assessments. Many agencies simply assign the highest level of supervision indicated by either scale. Others, by policy, will emphasize one scale over the other.

Both control and treatment philosophies represent legitimate correctional pursuits. However, reliance on a single approach serves neither the community nor the offender adequately, particularly in the juvenile area. A balanced approach of control and casework based on individual characteristics is essential to success in juvenile corrections. If correctional systems ignore the individual needs of juvenile offenders—whether through insensitivity or inadequacy—society will pay the price.

REFERENCES

Baird, S. Christopher. 1974. "Parole Prediction Report No. 3." Joliette, Ill.: Illinois Department of Corrections.

Baird, S. Christopher, and Richard Heinz. 1978. "Risk Assessment in Juvenile Probation and Aftercare." Madison, Wis.: Wisconsin Division of Corrections. Unpublished.

Baird, S. Christopher, Gregory M. Storrs, and Helen Connelly. 1984. *Classification of Juveniles in Corrections: A Model Systems Report.* Washington, D.C.: Arthur D. Little, Inc.

Hatalyn, Thomas V., and E.A. Wenk. 1974. "An Analysis of Classification for Young Adult Offenders." *NCCD Research*, Vol. 6. San Francisco, Calif.: National Council on Crime and Delinquency.

Jesness, Carl F., M. Bohnstedt, and M. Molof. 1973. *Sequential I-Level Classification.* Sacramento, Calif.: American Justice Institute.

National Institute of Corrections. 1981. "The Model Probation and Parole Management Program." Washington, D.C.: National Institute of Corrections.

Wenk, E.A., and R.L. Emerick. 1976. "Assaultive Youth: An Exploratory Study of the Assaultive Experience and the Assaultive Potential of CYA Wards." *Journal of Research of Crime and Delinquency*, Vol. 9, No. 2. San Francisco, Calif.: National Council on Crime and Delinquency.

S. Christopher Baird is director of the National Council on Crime and Delinquency—Midwest, Madison, Wisconsin.

Juvenile Justice
A Challenge for Change

Allen F. Breed

We do not need to change the juvenile justice system; rather, we need to become better advocates for children and youths and support principles conducive to their growth and development.

When one looks at the evolution of the juvenile justice system over the last ten years, it appears the combination of court attacks, standards that dramatically altered traditional operational methods, and a public climate of distrust caused a retrenchment in the strong voices of advocacy that historically existed in the juvenile justice field. The absence of advocacy is permitting a continual erosion of the principles that justified creation of the juvenile justice system and gave support to programs and approaches that have met the needs of many children and youths.

We do not need to change the juvenile justice system; rather, we need to become better advocates for children and youths and support the principles conducive to their personal growth and development. Unfortunately, we in juvenile corrections tend to "play it safe," and are reluctant to be too far out in front with our ideas and programs. Reasons for our reluctance are the public's attitude toward our charges, lack of a correctional morality, and the fact we operate in a very low-visibility environment in which only failures gain public attention. Most of all, however, it seems the basic problem is the absence of a philosophy and commitment to the things we should be doing, saying, and standing up and fighting for rather than just adhering to roles an ultra-conservative and vocal segment of our society demands we fulfill. We should be advocates for what we believe.

Advocacy itself is an unsatisfactory term, however. It has been borrowed, as many of our terms or concepts have, from the field of law. An advocate, by definition, is one who pleads the cause of another. Essentially, the characteristic of advocacy is a weak one. Because the advocate begins with a defensive stance and defends a position, the stance becomes reactionary rather than active in advancing a thought or program at his/her initiative. The juvenile justice system needs something more than a defensive speaker; it needs positive spokespersons for principles and programs that address the "best interests of the child" in the fullest sense of that term.

Tragically, we have become apologists for that term as juvenile crime and, more specifically, violent juvenile crime, rises to astronomical levels. We stand by as political opportunists change state statutes that called for rehabilitation, treatment, and the best interests of the child as the undergirding framework of this country's juvenile laws, and substitute terms like "protection of society" and "to ensure public safety."

Preserving the Juvenile Court

The juvenile court has been highly successful in meeting the needs of the majority of children brought into its jurisdiction. Why, in recent years then, has the juvenile court been confronted with virulent attacks by the media, law enforcement, and some professionals from both ends of the political spectrum? There appear to be three basic themes in the attacks:

- Lack of due process in court procedures and program management
- Overreach of the court into the lives of many children who, some believe, should not be entangled in any part of the justice system
- Public reaction to what appears to be lenient handling of serious and chronic juvenile offenders

There can be no question the juvenile court historically operated with minimal due process protections and, under the guise of "the best interests of the child," often violated the most basic rights of children, be they dependent, neglected, or delinquent. The *Gault* decision and its progeny put an end to such procedures and children under juvenile court jurisdiction have all the protections that adults do, with the exception of bail and trial by jury. A number of jurisdictions also are experimenting with these approaches as well.

In terms of court overreach into the lives of some children who perhaps should not be in a justice system program, the record appears to support that concern. As late as 1975, Congress found large numbers of status offenders and nonoffenders in adult jails, detention centers, and training schools. They further found many facilities and programs were seriously overcrowded and understaffed. The record clearly shows there were critical shortages of alternatives to formal court processing or placement in institutions.

Overreach of the juvenile court at this particular time in history was due to its trying to fill all of the social voids without the resources to do so. As an outgrowth of the congressional study, the Juvenile Justice Act was passed. Removal of many status offenders and nonoffenders from secure institutions was one of the most successful juvenile justice policy thrusts of the late 1970s and early 1980s. The juvenile court, however, continues to be the decision point and is often the only leverage ensuring that children and their families receive the most appropriate services and resources available.

The attack regarding the leniency of the juvenile court with serious and chronic juvenile offenders is a more complicated one. (Historically, society has had a benevolent attitude toward adolescent crime because most is of a nonserious nature and few juvenile offenders develop into career criminals. During the 1960s and 1970s, these attitudes changed as society dealt with a marked increase in serious juvenile crimes. Popular opinion shifted from tolerance of adolescent misbehavior to a philosophy that children and youths should be responsible for their actions and the consequences of those actions.)

The shift in public opinion, which is understandable and in many cases appropriate, has been accelerated by inflammatory and often inaccurate media coverage. It is not fair, however, to jump to the statement, "The juvenile court has failed." All crime is cyclical in nature, juvenile crime particularly so. There has been no empirical evidence to determine what causes the rises and falls. Studies have shown, though, compared with the criminal court, the juvenile court is more efficient and not more lenient with violent offenders. We also must recognize that 95 percent of the juvenile court's work load is with nonoffenders, status offenders, and minor offenders who do not belong in a criminal court.

The juvenile court has not failed. Because of an acute lack of resources, it would be more appropriate to say that it truly has never been tried. As advocates for the preservation of the juvenile court, we must develop strategies to both inform and educate the public about the realities of the juvenile crime problem. Currently there is a huge gap between trends in juvenile crime, actions of the juvenile court, and public perception of the problem. We should continue to refine the juvenile justice system to preserve due process protections while simultaneously developing and administering briefer, more effective, and more appropriate sanctions and services for the best interests of the child.

Youthful Offender Concept

A second principle we should advocate is the youthful offender concept. The original age of jurisdiction for the juvenile court extended to 21 years. As time went along and more older adolescents were involved in violent crimes, the upper age limit was reduced to 18, 17, then 16, with some states lowering the age to 14 for serious crimes. Two approaches developed over the years to handle the relatively small group of offenders too young to come under the jurisdiction of the adult court but too sophisticated in their criminality to be handled by the juvenile court. One was to use a transfer system allowing the juvenile court judge to waive to criminal court those individuals seen as too mature or too criminal to be tried by the juvenile court.

The other approach was a model developed by the American Law Institute in the early 1940s that called for a three-tier system of corrections—juvenile, youthful offender, and adult. The Youthful Offender Act, as it was originally known, was created to deal with selected offenders over 18 years of age and under 23 or 25 years who were seen by the courts as too old to be handled as juveniles and too young to be placed in an adult prison setting. This model was first developed in California and remains part of its Department of the Youth Authority. It rapidly spread to other states and was later enacted into legislation by Congress.

Unfortunately, many correctional jurisdictions having a youthful offender act failed to provide separate facilities and programs for this special age group and either incorporated them into juvenile facilities or placed them into adult prisons. Special requirements that existed in most youthful offender legislation made it administratively difficult to manage programs with different offender populations within a common facility. The result was most youthful offender programs were discontinued for management convenience reasons rather than for offender needs. The presence of youthful offenders in juvenile facilities further alarmed politicians who enacted legislation to restrict placement of this "in-between" age group with juvenile court wards.

As youthful offender programs were eliminated for administrative convenience and legislators continued to reduce the age of jurisdiction of the juvenile court and enlarge the scope of waiver provisions, the result has been an ever-increasing number of youthful offenders who may be too old for juvenile programs but are certainly too immature for today's prisons. As advocates for children and youths, we must support strongly the concept of a three-tier system that will not only provide a wider age distribution for the juvenile court, but provide a much richer, more diversified set of correctional options for the largest and most difficult age group to service, youthful offenders.

The third principle we should advocate is rehabilitation. Many in juvenile corrections have replaced the field's traditional optimism with the pessimistic view that what they do does not matter because it won't work anyway. Coupled with this attitudinal change about the poor odds of success came the popular wave of opinion that punishment of the offender should be an integral part of our responsibility as juvenile correctional practitioners. For some current juvenile corrections leaders to be speaking out in favor of punishment as if it were a new-found panacea would be laughable if it were not for the strong possibility their professional statements will be used by conservative law-and-order proponents to support sanctions that are even longer and harsher and to propose mandatory sentences. These attitudes will lead to artificial and inoperable rigidity in dealing with our clients, reduce needed resources, and bring about an even further decline in rehabilitative opportunities.

Perhaps, as some have claimed, rehabilitation of offenders was never achieved—perhaps it is unachievable—but the fact that it is sought provides leverage for enhancing the conditions that delinquent youths face.

Effective Diversion

As juvenile justice advocates, we also should support the principle of reducing penetration into the system. The word *diversion* is used to cover a multitude of activities. Diversion should mean no involvement in the justice system. It is this approach that raises the hackles of conservatives who resent the fact that no punishment takes place while raising the concerns of liberals that many of these children are diverted to non-justice programs for assistance and, in the process, "widen the net" of social control and label or stigmatize those whose behavior could best be ignored.

Research clearly demonstrates that most juvenile offenders follow careers dominated by minor offenses; there is a spontaneous remission that occurs in juvenile delinquents after the first, second, and third arrests; there is little progression from minor to more serious offenses, and there is little risk in ignoring early minor offending. We should concentrate our limited resources instead on the smaller number of serious or persistent offenders.

For many youngsters who come into contact with the justice system, nonintervention is good public policy. Many others would benefit from such services as employment counseling, family counseling, a relationship with a big brother or sister, substance abuse education, or even psychotherapy. Obviously, the challenge of our profession is to determine when this type of diversion is appropriate.

The two-pronged attack of "widening the net of social control" and stigmatization or labeling cannot be supported. Malcolm Klein, one of the most sophisticated commentators on juvenile diversion programs, stated "the labeling theory may rank as the most widely accepted unsupported proposition in criminology of the 1960s and 1970s. It fits the needs and biases of the field so well that careful empirical investigation has been largely bypassed."

The "widening the net" concept is a form of rhetoric by those who are suspicious of any agency intervention into the life of a child. The very emotional tone of the term—"dropping a net over a boy or girl"—invokes understandable concern and pity. But what if one substitutes the phrase "provide services to youngsters and their families where none was provided before" for "widens the net of social control"? Without the rhetoric and with the recognition that, for some children, merely behaving in certain ways without consequent social reaction may be the prime factor in producing a delinquent self-concept. Professionals should strongly support diversion, both in the form of nonintervention for some and problem-solving conflict resolution or provision of services germane to the nature of the deviance for others.

We should carefully reexamine our incarceration policy for juveniles. During the 1970s we witnessed a revolution in thought coupled with massive financial inducements to accomplish the deinstitutionalization of many of our juvenile offenders. However, today we find the following to be true:

- Thousands of children are detained in juvenile halls awaiting trial, although more than 75 percent of them are charged with property or lesser crimes and 80 percent of them will be released to the community after adjudication.
- Although juvenile crime has been falling for more than five years, more youths are confined in state training schools today than at any time in our history; 69 percent of those confined are guilty of property or lesser crimes.
- On any given day there are nearly 3,000 juveniles confined in state prisons.
- By the most conservative estimates, in any given year more than 100,000 juveniles are confined in the nation's jails and lock-ups.
- A sizable private sector residential system is developing, and it is responsible to massive insurance funds being made available for chemical dependency and as an alternative to justice system efforts to deinstitutionalize. In fact, our official deinstitutionalization efforts may well be offset by this new system.

As advocates for juvenile justice, we must speak out strongly for the principle of the "least coercive intervention necessary" because it is not happening. We must help the public understand most delinquents are not a threat to society, they do not need to be locked up awaiting trial, and there can be little justification for placing a young person in a jail or prison. Also, with the reduction in juvenile arrests, we cannot tolerate ever-increasing numbers confined in state training schools while at the same time reduce the resources made available to them. And in our efforts to use private sector resources, we cannot encourage duplication of confinement programs that, for sound public policy reasons, we are trying to reduce at government levels.

Reducing Causes of Social Failure

One last principle needing corrections' commitment is reducing causes of social failure. We no longer can content ourselves as professionals in only expressing a concern about the children who come into the juvenile justice system. We must advocate changes in society's systems that contribute to the development of the failures we receive. Conservative estimates by informed sources suggest social systems operating in 1984 produced a social casualty rate of about 25 percent. A loss factor of this level cannot be tolerated in a nation predicated on equality and justice.

A social casualty is a student who comes out of our educational system unable to read or unable to speak the language of the country. It is the child with birth defects due to the mother not receiving adequate medical care or nutrition. It is the victim of child abuse. The social casualty is also the youngster who grows up accepting rats, lice, and other vermin as a natural and inevitable part of the environment that nurtures him. It is the product of a society not currently geared to protect the poorest among us regardless of the political party in power. And, certainly, it is the children and youths with whom we work. In this sense, juvenile justice advocacy must cover a broader spectrum of concern and deal with issues that touch upon the delivery practices of all human services systems.

Correctional systems, if they are to correct, must take more positive positions in favor of things we know are important in modifying and changing the behavior of those we find within our care. More importantly, we must face up to the issue that crime and delinquency are truly the result of interactions between the individual and the environment. Almost all programs still are predicated on the "sick model," which establishes the fault and blame for behavior entirely within the individual rather than the individual in interaction with a series of circumstances in society over which he/she may have relatively little control. We in corrections must, in concert with an informed citizenry, work to reduce those social conditions that add new offenders to the juvenile justice population.

A positive youth advocacy program is needed to speak out in behalf of not just the children of the juvenile justice system, but indeed, speak out in behalf of the rights and needs of all children and youths. We who receive society's failures and rejects have a responsibility to develop greater awareness of these needs; greater recognition of the interrelatedness of the juvenile justice, child welfare, mental health, education, and newly emerging chemical dependency systems; and a willingness to advocate for necessary resources and programs. If our professional efforts to reduce crime and delinquency are limited to our institutions and field programs, it will be like people trying to divert the flow of the mighty Mississippi with buckets as it enters the Gulf of Mexico. We must go upstream and begin our diversion of crime by attacking the causes of social failure.

The challenge for change in the juvenile justice arena, then, is to recognize the system works and to strengthen that system by becoming true advocates of the principles underlying a specialized system of justice for children and youths and, above all, to reaffirm through our personal advocacy this nation's commitment to children embodied in the United Nations Declaration of the Rights of Children, which reads:

> The child shall enjoy special protection, and shall be given opportunities and facilities, by law and by other means, to enable him to develop physically, mentally, morally, spiritually and socially in health and normal manner and in conditions of freedom and dignity. In the enactment of laws for this purpose, the best interest of the child shall be the paramount consideration.

Allen F. Breed is a criminal justice consultant in San Andreas, California, and vice president of the ACA.

Training Officers in Juvenile Detention

Melvin Brown Jr., Ph.D.

Training for juvenile detention child care personnel should rely very heavily on in-service training and staff development programs that do more than teach new staff 'what to do and when to do it.'

Training juvenile detention personnel is vitally important because juvenile detention facility staff must fill myriad roles in the lives of the children who are detained, and they must perform these roles well. In order to design a successful training program for detention personnel, the following roles of the child care worker in a juvenile detention facility must be examined.

• *Security Officer*—Juvenile detention is defined by the National Council on Crime and Delinquency as "the temporary care of children in physically restricting facilities pending court disposition or transfer to another jurisdiction or agency." Thus, one of the roles the child care staff must fill is that of security officer. This includes searching the children and their rooms for contraband and maintaining control over tools and recreational equipment that might be used as weapons. Providing security also means being alert to possible escape attempts and knowing how to prevent them, as well as protecting children against their own uncontrolled actions.

• *Counselor*—If intake is properly controlled, children who are detained are the community's most troublesome and disturbed offenders. They are detained when belief in themselves has been shattered. Their anxiety is often expressed by extreme indifference, open hostility, or a veneer of cooperation. These children range from being extremely withdrawn to extremely aggressive, making it a necessity for child care workers to have a working knowledge of adolescent behavior and behavioral intervention techniques. In dealing with detained children, good interpersonal and crisis counseling skills are essential.

• *Disciplinarian*—Many detained children display acting-out behavior. Many are hostile toward authority of all types. The behavior of these children is not easily redirected, yet punitive measures make it worse. It is the responsibility of the detention worker to turn the acting-out behavior of children into positive learning experiences. The purpose of discipline should not be to increase the controlling behavior of staff, but to build the self-control of the youths in detention.

• *Recorder of Behavior*—Writing behavior observation reports is also an important responsibility of child care staff. These reports can affect a child's placement and can be instrumental in solving personality problems. As a result of their daily interaction with the children, detention workers usually know them far better than a probation officer or caseworker. This knowledge carries with it a heavy responsibility because it affects each child's future. It is important that child care staff be able to write objective, accurate reports on observed behavior.

• *Activity Coordinator*—Another function that requires a large amount of the child care worker's time and effort is coordinating and supervising the daily activity program. The child care worker's responsibilities often include not only ensuring the children are in their scheduled daily activities but also assisting in or providing leadership for the activities. Generally, the child care worker serves as an assistant teacher when his/her group is in the classroom and as a leader during recreational activities. During recreation time, the child care worker teaches the rules of the game and value of team work. During free time, the child care worker helps structure time to reduce boredom and its constant companion, acting-out behavior.

Other factors affecting the training program for detention personnel are inherent in the operation of the detention facility itself. Because the detention facility must operate 24 hours a day, seven days a week, it is practically impossible to provide training for all personnel and provide supervision for the detained children at the same time. While it is difficult, it is not impossible to provide staff training to improve the skills required to meet job demands successfully.

Training for juvenile detention child care personnel should rely very heavily on in-service training and staff development programs. The training program should do more than teach new staff "what to do and when to do it." It should develop a professional attitude based on an increasing knowledge of children's behavior and counteract any tendency toward mechanical custodial procedures in child-staff relationships. The training program must constantly clarify the philosophy and objectives of the juvenile detention facility and focus on specific practices. It also should create a process of staff development that helps those working directly with children to:

- Develop a greater understanding of themselves in relation to the behavior problems of the children for whom they are responsible
- Develop a greater understanding of normal as well as abnormal child and adolescent behavior
- Gain a wider view of their job in relation to the work of the court, the juvenile justice system, and other public and private child care agencies in the community

Along with the above, the training should include training in the practical routines of the job, training in specific activities, and development of special skills and methods for handling behavior incidents.

Design for Learning

Someone has said that designing a learning experience is analagous to planning a trip. It involves three things: 1) setting the goal, or destination, 2) determining where the travelers/learners are, or their departure point, and 3) specifying a sequence of events that will enable the travelers/learners to move from their point of departure to their destination. Each juvenile detention administrator will need to determine what skills or knowledge the staff under his/her supervision should possess to be effective child care workers. Each employee brings to the job different skills in different degrees. Therefore, training should be designed to move learners from the level of knowledge or skills possessed to the level they need to do an effective job.

Much of the training of juvenile detention personnel will, by necessity, take place on the job. This does not mean, however, simply giving employees their assignments, telling them what to do, and leaving them to do it. Effective on-the-job training involves an orientation that spells out the philosophy and objectives of the juvenile detention facility and role of the child care staff. A new worker should be assigned to work with an experienced worker who most nearly meets the criteria of the ideal child care worker. That worker can model the behavior and attitude the new worker is to acquire. On-the-job training will be even more effective if the new worker can work with more than one experienced staff member. By working with various staff members the new worker observes various approaches to handling the same problems and can adopt those most comfortable to him/her.

Printed material taken from books, journals, and magazines or developed by a staff member can be beneficial if it is short, well written, and relevant. Printed material can serve as the launching pad for discussions conducted at regularly scheduled staff training sessions. Excellent material is available on behavior observation reports, searching techniques, and behavioral intervention strategies.

Staff Training Meetings

Few things, if any, serve the purpose of training better than well-planned, regularly scheduled staff training sessions. As mentioned above, previously distributed printed material can serve as the basis for session discussions. This is also a time when problem areas can be discussed, giving the new or less experienced child care staff an opportunity to see how more experienced staff have handled or would handle similar situations.

Staff training sessions also provide opportunity for new staff to raise questions about how situations might be handled or be given feedback on how they handled a situation. In one juvenile detention facility, if there had been a disturbance, escape, or major incident of any kind, that became the topic of discussion for a staff training session. The staff member involved in the incident first described the event, the events that preceded it, and what actions were taken by him/her or other staff members. The staff member was then asked what he/she would do differently if the same situation arose again. Other staff members asked questions.

Following the presentation by involved staff members, the rest of the staff were asked, "What would you have done had you been the staff member on duty?" This gives an opportunity for staff to voice support for proper actions taken by the staff members on duty and to suggest other approaches that might have been taken. After discussing approaches to dealing with the incident as it actually happened, the question was raised, "How could this situation have been avoided?" This, again, provides an opportunity to view various approaches to the problem and for staff to get feedback from each other.

When first introduced, this approach is quite threatening to staff members, but if it is conducted on a regular basis, in such a way that is interpreted as a learning experience and not as "being called on the carpet," staff members become very open in their sharing and find the experience very beneficial. As one staff member said, "There are enough mistakes to go around; there is no need to repeat one made by someone else." This is an excellent way for staff members to learn from experience, both theirs and others.

Scheduling Training Sessions

Providing staff training sessions on a regular basis can be quite difficult. However, there are various ways of providing training opportunities. One approach is to schedule training sessions at the change of shifts. For example, if the facility follows the traditional 7 A.M.–3 P.M., 3 P.M.–11 P.M., 11 P.M.–7 A.M. staffing pattern, training could be scheduled from 2:30–3:30, or 2:15–3:45, depending upon the amount of time required. One facility using this approach held a training session on Monday one week, Tuesday the next, Wednesday the next, etc. When the training session was on Friday, there would be no training session the following week. The rotation of days would begin all over again the next Monday.

To provide this system of training it would be necessary to enlist assistance of academic, supervisory, and support personnel to provide supervision of the children in detention during the training session. A similar approach is having the trainer present two staff training sessions back to back. The training session for the 3 P.M.–11 P.M. staff would take place at 2 P.M. At 3:00 they would go on duty, and the 7

A.M.–3 P.M. staff would have their training session. With this approach, 11 P.M. staff can choose which session they would rather attend. Either approach to a regularly scheduled training session has weaknesses, but they are outweighed by the advantages of an ongoing staff training program. Compensatory time cost is the greatest drawback to this approach but is minuscule when compared to the benefits.

Often individuals read, or are told, how to do something, but because opportunities to practice it are not provided, they fail to learn to do it properly. Opportunities to practice procedures under supervision need to be provided so bad habits do not develop. One procedure for combining the previous two methods of training—use of printed materials and regularly scheduled staff training sessions—with providing opportunities to practice a skill under supervision has been effectively used in one detention facility.

At a regular staff training session, printed material on searching techniques was distributed. During the following session, the material was discussed, and staff practiced searching each other. Then the trainer, who had hidden contraband in numerous places in his clothing before the session, asked one of the staff members to search him. After the search, the trainer revealed all the contraband not found by the staff member, not to embarrass the staff member (this was made clear), but to point out the importance of doing a thorough search.

The same approach can be taken with searching rooms. Before the staff meeting, a number of rooms are placed off limits to children and staff. Contraband is hidden in the rooms, and a list compiled of what was hidden and where it was hidden. At the staff meeting, staff members are directed to go search the designated rooms.

A number of opportunities for learning present themselves. First, staff members can see other staff members looking in places they had not thought of looking. Secondly, following the room search, it is discovered that all of the objects hidden by the trainer were not found. This gives an opportunity to point out some areas being overlooked by the staff in their searches. Thirdly, on some occasions, staff will find contraband not hidden by the trainer. This points out the importance of conducting frequent room searches.

Practice in other child care responsibilities can be provided through similar approaches. Never overlook the value of practice in a training program.

Programmed Instruction

Another method that can be extremely beneficial in staff training is using programmed instruction materials. Programmed instruction has the advantage of allowing staff to learn on their own at their own pace. Programmed instruction is a method whereby learners are given information in coherent, interrelated steps that cause them to use knowledge as it is gained, thus reinforcing the use of the knowledge.

Many procedures used in juvenile detention facilities could be taught through this method. Through programmed instruction, child care workers can master the knowledge at home in their spare time. While this approach to training of juvenile detention child care staff is rare at the present time, it is an excellent approach, and does not have many of the disadvantages (e.g., finding a way to get all of the staff together for training) of the previously mentioned methods.

There are many effective approaches to training juvenile detention facility staff. Some methods of instruction are more suited to one type of material than another. Each method should be tailored to the situation, bringing to bear every relevant resource in creative ways and making the training rewarding to staff and instructors.

Melvin Brown Jr., Ph.D., is director of the Montgomery County, Texas, Juvenile Probation and Adult Probation departments, Conroe, Texas.

Turning Point Youth Services:
A Delinquency Prevention Project

M. Amos Clifford

In developing programs and treatment approaches for preventing and intervening in delinquency, it is important to have a 'road map'—a policymaking position based on sound research.

Turning Point Youth Services (TPYS) is a delinquency prevention project located in Visalia, California, an agricultural city located at the base of the Sierra Nevada Mountains in the San Joaquin Valley. TPYS focuses on the earliest stages of delinquency: chronic family conflict, vandalism, petty theft, experimental substance abuse, and other behavior problems. Most probation referrals to the program are through a juvenile diversion project. Rarely are youths referred by the courts. Program staff prefer that youths are referred in the earlier stages; problems can be addressed more effectively and with greater cost effectiveness that way.

The program's counseling emphasis is on family therapy, but individual and group therapy are often included in treatment plans. Other program components include parenting classes, assistance to schools in developing prevention programs based on promoting positive behaviors and skills, and a recreation component that helps youths develop self-esteem, communication skills, and greater self-confidence. Turning Point works closely with a variety of related agencies, including schools, probation, and grass-roots parent groups such as Toughlove and The Chemical People.

Tracey (not her real name) telephones to inform her counselor that she, once again, is suspended from the continuation high school she attends. Like last time, this suspension is for fighting. She is angry at the school dean who she says didn't listen when she tried to explain that she fought in self-defense. She is angry at her alcoholic mother who was obviously under the influence when she met with the dean. And she is afraid of how her probation officer is going to react— will the P.O. really put her in the hall for a month as threatened?

While these are the pressing issues on Tracey's mind, her counselor sees a broader issue. The counselor's concern is helping Tracey learn the skills she needs to escape a lifestyle of addiction, marginal criminality, and low achievement. In short, how can her current crisis be used to help her "grow up"?

The question of how to help kids grow up summarizes the task of community delinquency prevention efforts. In developing programs and treatment approaches for preventing and intervening in delinquency, it is important to have a "road map" —a policymaking position based on sound research—to guide the myriad decisions that go into helping troubled youths.

While researching delinquent and drug-abusing youths in the late 1970s, Glenn and Warner (1982) identified seven skills or characteristics that can be taught to prevent delinquency:

- Identifying with viable role models
- Identifying with and responsibility for family processes
- Developing faith in personal resources for solving problems
- Developing awareness of and control over feelings and related thinking
- Developing skills for dealing with others
- Developing situational skills
- Developing good judgment and decision-making skills

These skills provide TPYS with its road map. By promoting them, the program encourages normal, healthy development in troubled youths. Each characteristic or skill is examined below, with a look at how the program helps youths develop in these areas.

Viable Role Models

Tracey's father has been absent since she was an infant, her mother and grandmother are alcoholics, and her older sister is a heroin addict, supporting her habit by prostitution. Like many youths, Tracey bases her estimation of what is possible for her to achieve on examples found in her family. An effective prevention or corrections program will link Tracey with alternative role models. Often, the program counselor can be a role model, but teachers, peer counselors, probation officers, bosses, or others can serve well in this function.

A key to effective impact as a role model is the willingness to develop a significant relationship with the youth. TPYS includes program components that facilitate this. An example is the program's Summer Alternatives Project. On this project, staff take youths on three- to five-day camping, backpacking, and mountaineering outings. According to one counselor, "Living with these kids 24 hours a day for that long really makes you get to know each other. I'd never learn half as much about them just by having counseling appointments." Staff members have many opportunities to model alternative behaviors in response to events ranging from dividing chores, to handling conflicts, to taking the time to listen.

Robert K. Meyers boys' camp, north of the county seat of Visalia, also connects probationers with alternative resources and role models. Turning Point and other agencies hold special educational and therapeutic group meetings with the boys on a four-week rotating basis. A key program goal is connecting the boys with a variety of people from agencies in their community—role models—who can assist them after they are released from camp.

Families like Tracey's are of major concern to prevention specialists and counselors. Ideally, parents like Tracey's are identified and treated before children suffer serious damage. Parenting classes can be one method of accomplishing this. But in cases involving alcoholic or abusive parents, such problems must be addressed first. When parents will not participate in treatment, the child must be worked with individually.

Treatment is not limited to dealing with Tracey's accumulated baggage of distressed feelings. Inoculating her against further negative effects of living in a difficult family environment is one goal of treatment. She must come to recognize her dilemma for what it is, reorient herself to personal goals, and connect with viable resources outside the family. These resources can include counseling or self-help groups such as Alanon, clubs, friends, or families. They may become a surrogate "family" providing important support for weathering future family stress while teaching how to function in a family system.

Solving Problems

Tracey, accustomed to 30-minute television episodes showing major conflicts among people resolved by slam-bang fights, tried the same solution to solve her problem with her classmate. Of course, this approach led to further complications and bigger problems. When her counselor asked her to suggest other ways she might have behaved, Tracey was unable to think of any.

Conflict resolution is one area in which many predelinquent youths lack skills. One of two unrealistic approaches usually is tried by these youths: the domineering approach or the passive approach. The frustration inevitably encountered as a result of either of these approaches further erodes confidence in personal problem-solving skills. To grow in this area, youths need solid educational programs and real problem-solving opportunities.

One such program is the Social Skills Class taught by TPYS staff in area junior high schools. These schools have segregated groups of high-risk youths into "learning opportunity" classes. In these classes, TPYS staff members use process-oriented small groups to teach two major skills: how to say no and still keep your friends (most of the time), and how to earn and accept compliments. Many of the exercises used in these groups present problems students can practice for similar real-life episodes.

Mary Ann Pentz, Ph.D., cites evidence this approach can be effective in preventing delinquency. Writing about drug abuse she states, "There is substantial evidence that social skills training can reduce drug-use levels, increase periods of abstinence, and prevent relapse to problem behavior" (Pentz 1983).

Glenn and Warner write that "intrapersonal skills are developed by having four things happen. The child must: 1) have experiences..., 2) identify what was experienced, 3) analyze how it occurred, and 4) generalize that learning to other situations" (Glenn and Warner 1982). To help Tracey in this area, a rock-climbing class was incorporated into her treatment plan.

Faced with the challenge of climbing a vertical rock, Tracey's response was typical of most delinquent (and many nondelinquent) youths. She insisted, "I can't do that...that's too hard." Her fear interfered with her ability to conceive of herself as a capable individual. This is an example of limiting self-concept due to poor intrapersonal skills.

With some coaxing, Tracey found courage to struggle with the challenge. She eventually succeeded. As a result, her perception of her capabilities was enhanced. When she recalled her initial self-doubt and compared it with her ultimate success, a powerful metaphor was created. She now can compare future episodes of self-doubt with "the time I climbed the rock...I didn't think I could do that either, but when I tried, I found I could." She learned to manage feelings of self-doubt by thinking challenges through.

This approach usually is most effective when integrated with complementary experiences. Turning Point often uses a rock-climbing field trip as a final session for a social skills development class.

Interpersonal Skills

When Tracey is angry, she fights. As a result, her relationships with other people suffer. Like most delinquent youths, Tracey blames her poor relationships on "the other guy."

During the course of counseling, Tracey will interact with many people. Each of these interactions presents an opportunity for the counselor to review some basic questions with Tracey, such as: "When you said what you did, how did she react? When you did that to her, did she react in the way you wanted her to? What other words or actions could you have used? Would that have changed the outcome?" As a result, Tracey will learn to evaluate her relationships from the perspective of personal responsibility. She will try new behaviors, becoming less rigid and stereotyped in her approaches to relationships. Skills she learns by this process will result in more satisfactory interaction with others.

To many delinquents, events that affect them seem random, guided by fate, luck, or some malicious "system." This idea supports "copping out." "Look, it's not my fault" is a typical refrain. When children learn they can influence many life events, they are more likely to accept responsibility for the consequences of their behavior.

In 1983, seeking alternatives to five-day suspensions for students caught under the influence of drugs on campus, Visalia Unified School District worked out a unique arrangement with TPYS. Suspended students were encouraged to enroll immediately in counseling at TPYS. In return, the district would consider cutting the suspension to three days. But to earn this, the student had to apply for readmission.

TPYS counselors used this as an opportunity to help these youths understand how specific behaviors affect their interaction with institutions. Students were coached in assertion techniques. They then approached the dean and petitioned for readmission, based on evidence of attending counseling. These students were readmitted. They experienced firsthand the cause-and-effect relationship between their actions and their ability to achieve a specific goal within the institution.

Learning from Consequences

Most delinquency prevention programs place great emphasis on developing decision-making skills. Accountability is a key to effective decision making. A classic example is the forgotten lunchbox. Should the parent make a special journey to school to see that Johnny gets lunch, or should Johnny go hungry today as a result of his poor judgment? The parent who takes Johnny the lunchbox personally takes on the consequences of his behavior and steals a good learning opportunity from him. Missing a lunch and similar natural consequences are still the best way to develop this important skill.

Often, caring counselors, parents, and probation officers interfere with development of this skill by "taking the lunch to school." A probation officer who doesn't follow up on threatened consequences for violations or a counselor who intervenes with school officials on behalf of a client are examples. A better response in most instances is to allow the child to experience the consequences of his/her decision and then to help him/her think it through objectively.

Basic life skills training provides a road map to effective delinquency prevention by helping children grow up. The outcome of life skills competence is the child's improved ability to mature into a productive adult.

These skills have important applications to delinquency prevention. Development of these skills also should be emphasized in the treatment of the institutionalized delinquent. Obviously, these skills are learned with less effort in the earlier stages and, from the agency's point of view, with more cost effectiveness. However, programs that address these learning needs in juvenile halls, camps, and other youth corrections institutions will probably be more successful in reducing recidivism than programs that do not. Well-planned and coordinated, cooperative interaction with a variety of community resource agencies also is essential to effective delinquency prevention.

REFERENCES

Glenn, H. Stephen, and Joel W. Warner. 1982. *Developing Capable Young People.* Hurst, Tex.: Humansphere, Inc.

Pentz, Mary Ann, Ph.D. 1983. "Prevention of Adolescent Substance Abuse Through Social Skill Development," *Preventing Adolescent Drug Abuse: Intervention Strategies,* National Institute on Drug Abuse Research Monograph No. 47. Rockville, Md.: Department of Health and Human Services.

M. Amos Clifford is program director of Turning Point Youth Services, Turning Point of Central California, Visalia, California.

Who Is the Serious Juvenile Offender?

Jeanne C. Cyriaque

The serious offenders in Illinois' juvenile institutions all share characteristics justifying their commitment to state facilities.

During recent years the juvenile justice system has been forced to address the issues of chronicity and violence as youth involvement in crime has escalated. Public sentiment and legislation have demanded harsher treatment of serious juvenile offenders, resulting in a change of emphasis from rehabilitative models to more punitive, "get tough" models. Corresponding with this change, corrections professionals have witnessed dramatic changes in the profiles of juveniles committed to state institutions.

In Illinois, juvenile corrections has responded to the serious offender concept by 1) developing a classification system that sorts the population by factors associated with risk and needs, 2) implementing an automated management information system specifically tailored for juveniles that provides data for key decisions related to programs and resource allocation, and 3) assessing the population through research studies based on admissions cohorts.

The Illinois Department of Corrections (IDOC) cohort study examined admissions to the juvenile division during 1978 and 1979. The effort involved review of 1,246 master files and captured key criminal histories, backgrounds, correctional efforts, and outcome measures. This article discusses characteristics of the cohort by examining six offender subgroups that differentiate property, violent, and sex offenders. These include burglars, thieves, armed robbers, aggravated batterers, sex offenders, and murderers.

Juvenile Burglars

Burglars in the admissions cohort totaled 426, or 34 percent of all cases examined. The burglar subgroup was 56.1 percent white, 35 percent black, 8.5 percent Hispanic, and 0.4 percent other races. While burglars represented the largest offender group, female commitments for this offense were minimal (1.4 percent). Two-thirds of all burglars were committed to IDOC solely for this offense, while the remainder were committed for several offenses. Burglary represented the most serious offense.

Family stability at commitment was assessed by reviewing social history data and staff meeting records. Families characterized as disorganized had problems that appeared to contribute to youths' current difficulties. The "major disorganization" category included families that had rejected youths, leaving them with no placement upon release. Among burglars, 10.9 percent came from severely disorganized families and 35.8 percent had experienced some disorganization in the home.

Extent of neglect and abuse in the cohort was measured by documentation from the committing court and also through self-reported information noted in the master file. The burglar subgroup had documented neglect in 6.8 percent of the cases and documented abuse in 3.7 percent. Neglect was self-reported among 8.4 percent of the burglars, and abuse was cited by 8.5 percent of the youths. White burglars were twice as likely to cite abuse and neglect as contributing to their delinquency than were minority burglars.

Examination of mental health needs among burglars showed 23.7 percent had histories of mental health problems before commitment. Approximately 4 percent of the burglars had learning disabilities, and 1.2 percent were retarded. Psychological evaluations were requested for 31 percent of the burglars during institutionalization.

Burglars represented the most unstable population among all offender subgroups when escape history was measured. Nearly 44 percent of all juveniles committed for burglary attempted escapes from IDOC facilities, detention centers, or residential centers.

Offense records included prior offense information, which was coded in the "history of dangerousness" variable. Burglars with violent offense histories totaled 203 (48.6 percent). Among burglars with violent histories, 64 percent were minor or situational, while 26 percent involved some injury or threat to the victim. Only 9.4 percent of the burglars had three or more violent offenses in their history, and 0.5 percent were gratuitous violent incidents in which death or serious injury occurred.

Burglars tend to begin their criminal careers between the ages of 12 and 14 (40.5 percent). This age of onset was most common among all offender subgroups.

Both probation and parole violations were examined for offender subgroups. Property offenders (burglars and thieves) were more likely to have violations than violent offenders. For the burglar subgroup, 30.7 percent had one previous probation violation and 19.7 percent had two or more documented violations. While on parole, 17.8 percent had one violation, and 14.1 percent had two or more. Burglars averaged between 7 and 12 months of institutionalization (40.2 percent).

Juvenile Thieves

The "thieves" offender subgroup comprised 202 cases, or 16.2 percent of the admissions cohort. Similar to characteristics of the burglar along racial lines, this group was composed of 51.5 percent white youths, 44.1 percent black, 3.5 percent Hispanic, and 1.0 percent other races. White youths accounted for more than half of the property offender subgroup. Females comprised 4.5 percent of the thief subgroup. Juveniles were committed to IDOC for theft as the single instant offense in 79.2 percent of the cases.

Some family disorganization was noted among 32.3 percent of the thieves, and 13.3 percent had severely disorganized families. Severe family disorganization was more common among thieves than burglars. Neglect was documented among 8.4 percent of the thief subgroup and cited in 10.9 percent of the cases. Neglect was documented among thieves more often than any offender subgroup. Child abuse was documented in 5.4 percent of the cases and cited by youths in an additional 8.9 percent.

Approximately 29 percent of the offenders committed for theft had histories of mental health problems. Learning disabilities were found in 3 percent of this subgroup, and evidence of retardation existed for 1.5 percent of them. Psychological evaluations were requested for 37.1 percent of the thieves. No significant differences were found for these mental health variables among both property offender groups.

Similar to burglars, thieves escaped from facilities more frequently than violent offenders. Escape attempts were noted in 38.9 percent of the cases. History of dangerousness was found among 113 thieves, or 55.9 percent. Violent offenses that were minor or situational accounted for 58.4 percent, while 30.1 percent involved some injury or threat to the victim. Three or more violent offenses were found in 11.5 percent of the thief subgroup, but no gratuitous violence was found in this group.

Age at first arrest was between 12 and 14 for 39.8 percent of the thieves. An additional 33 percent had age of onset at 11 or under; thieves had proportionately more cases with age of onset at 11 than any other offender subgroup.

Probation violations were similar to those of burglars in that 24.7 percent had one violation recorded, and 20.3 percent had two or more violations. Parole violations were common among thieves, with 24.2 percent of the subgroup having one violation, and 16.3 percent having two or more violations. Thieves averaged between 7 and 12 months institutionalization for 45.5 percent of the cases.

Juvenile Robbers

Juvenile robbers comprised 178 cases in the admissions cohort (14.3 percent). This subgroup included 96 armed robbers and 82 cases of simple robbery. Racial composition of this offender group totaled 69.7 percent black, 19.1 percent white, and 11.2 percent Hispanic. Black youths were committed for robbery offenses more frequently than any racial group, while white youths were the least visible among robbers. Females were committed for robbery in 6.7 percent of the cases. Similar to the property offender, robbers were committed for one offense in over two-thirds of all cases.

Some family disorganization was found in 47.2 percent of the robbery subgroup, while major disorganization was noted in 3.1 percent of the cases. Robbers had less major disorganization in the family than any offender group. Neglect was cited by 7.9 percent of the robbers and documented in the court records for 1.7 percent. Robbers, as a group, had the least abuse documentation of any offender subgroup.

Histories of mental health problems were noted among 20.8 percent of the robbers. Learning disabilities were found among 4.5 percent of this subgroup, and retardation existed for 1.7 percent. Psychological evaluations were requested for 28.6 percent, the lowest proportion of evaluations for any of the groups.

Escapes were attempted at least one or more times for 26.2 percent of the robbers. Robbers differed considerably from property offenders on the history of dangerousness variable with more than 80 percent of the robbers having dangerous histories. While property offenders' violent histories often were situational, 53.8 percent of the robbers had prior violent incidents involving some injury or threat, 19.3 percent had three or more violent offenses, and 2.1 percent were incidents of gratuitous violence.

The most common age at first arrest for robbers was between 12 and 14 (42.7 percent). Thirty-two percent of the robbers were between 15 and 16 at first arrest, and 25.3 percent were 11 or younger.

One probation violation was noted among 20.8 percent of the robbers, and two or more violations were recorded for 11.2 percent. Robbers were institutionalized between 7 and 12 months in 36.4 percent of the cases, between 13 and 18 months in 30.9 percent, and more than 18 months in 33 percent. Length of stay was often determined by institutional behavior for this group, accounting for the wide variation in average institutionalization.

Juvenile Batterers

Juveniles committed to IDOC for aggravated or simple battery totaled 145, or 11.6 percent of the cohort. The batterer subgroup was 48.6 percent black, 32.6 percent white, 18.1 percent Hispanic, and 0.7

percent other races. More Hispanic youths were represented in this subgroup than any other offender group. A similar pattern emerged for female participation, as 9 percent of the batterers were female. Batterers were committed for more than one offense in 43.4 percent of the cases.

Family disorganization was similar to property offenders' profiles, in that 36.9 percent of the batterers' families had some disorganization, and 13.5 percent were described as severely disorganized.

Neglect was cited by 9 percent of the batterers and documented for an additional 7.6 percent. Child abuse was cited by 8.3 percent of the batterers and documented in 4.8 percent.

Histories of mental health problems were identified for 36.5 percent of the batterers. This subgroup, along with sex offenders, had histories of mental health problems far more frequently than other subgroups. Learning disabilities were documented in 4.8 percent of this subgroup, and evidence of retardation was found in 3.4 percent of the batterers. Psychological evaluations were requested for 41.4 percent of the batterers.

Juvenile batterers attempted escape as often as property offenders—37.9 percent of the recorded attempts were by batterers. Batterers identified as having dangerous histories totaled 125, or 86 percent of this subgroup. As the records indicated, 47.2 percent had violent histories characterized by some injury or threat, and 17.6 percent had three or more violent incidents in their offense histories.

Batterers' average age at first arrest was between 12 and 14 (45.1 percent). At least one probation violation was documented for 27.6 percent, and 17.2 percent had two or more probation violations. One parole violation was documented for 18.6 percent, while 14.5 percent of the batterer subgroup had two or more violations. The average period of institutionalization for batterers was between 7 and 12 months.

Juvenile Sex Offenders and Murderers

The sex offender subgroup consisted of 53 juveniles, or 4.2 percent of the cohort. A similar racial pattern to the armed robber subgroup existed for this subgroup, who were primarily rapists. The sex offenders were 65.4 percent black, 25 percent white, and 9.6 percent Hispanic.

Sex offenders, more than any other subgroup, were committed for more than one offense in over half of the cases. This finding suggests that other crimes, such as robbery, often occur along with commission of sexual offenses.

Unlike the property offender, the sex offender's family was characterized as stable for half of the cases. Major disorganization was noted in only 8.3 percent of the sexual offenders' histories. While child neglect was cited by 18.9 percent of this subgroup, it was documented in only 1.9 percent, the lowest percentage of any subgroup. Child abuse was cited by 9.4 percent of the sex offenders, while none of these cases were documented. This finding suggests that both neglect and abuse may exist more for this offender group, but it is rarely documented by the justice system.

Prior histories of mental health problems were noted in 38.5 percent of the sex offender case files. Both batterers and sex offenders had such histories more often than other subgroups. Learning disabilities were found in 5.7 percent of the sex offenders, and psychological evaluations were requested for 52.8 percent of this subgroup.

One or more escapes were attempted by 18.9 percent of the sex offenders. This management problem was not as extensive as property offenders' escapes. Similar to other violent offenders, 85 percent of the sex offenders had offense histories noted by violent incidents. Nearly 29 percent of the sex offenders had three or more violent incidents before the committed offense, and 6.7 percent were gratuitous violence incidents. More than any other offender subgroup examined, the sex offenders tended to establish patterns of violence in their offense histories.

Age at first arrest for this subgroup was between 15 and 16 for 43.5 percent. Both sex offenders and murderers tended to begin their criminal careers at later ages than property offenders. One probation violation was found for 30.2 percent of the sex offenders, while 3.8 percent violated probation two or more times. Seventeen percent of the sex offenders violated parole once; 18.9 percent had two or more parole violations. Approximately 52 percent of the sex offenders remained institutionalized more than 18 months.

The IDOC cohort included 69 murderers (5.5 percent). Most in this subgroup were juveniles committed for murder or attempted murder.

Thirteen offenders committed for voluntary or involuntary man-slaughter were included in this offender subgroup.

Racial composition of this offender subgroup was 49.3 percent black, 36.2 percent white, and 14.5 percent Hispanic. Four percent of the murderers were female. Murderers were committed for more than one offense in 44.8 percent of the cases.

Similar to the sex offender, murderers came from stable family settings in 53.3 percent of the cases. Only 6.7 percent of the murderers' families were severely disorganized. Neglect was cited and documented among 2.9 percent of the murderers. Murderers, more than any other offender group, had documented abuse histories in 8.7 percent of the cases.

Mental health problems were identified prior to commitment for 26.1 percent of the murderers. Learning disabilities were documented in 5.8 percent of this subgroup, and psychological evaluations were requested for 42 percent of these offenders.

Escapes were attempted by 14.5 percent of the murderers, the lowest percentage of all offender subgroups. Approximately 65 percent of the murderers had violent histories. Of the cases with dangerousness histories, 55.6 percent involved some injury or threat, while 17.8 percent had three or more violent offenses. Gratuitous violence was found in 4.4 percent of this subgroup.

Similar to sex offenders, age at first arrest was between 15 and 16 for 43.5 percent. At least one probation violation was found in 18.8 percent of this subgroup; 8.7 percent had two or more probation violations. One parole violation was noted for 2.9 percent, while 21.7 percent had two or more parole violations. Nearly 70 percent of the murderers were institutionalized for 18 months or longer.

Tailoring Programs and Resources

The serious offenders in Illinois' juvenile institutions all share characteristics that justify their commitment to state facilities. Both property and violent offenders in Illinois are youths for whom other intervention efforts have failed. The most notable differences between the two groups lie in the instability versus dangerousness factors.

This discussion has highlighted property offenders as juveniles who are more likely to escape, begin their criminal careers at age 11 or younger, fail to respond to community intervention, have family and mental health problems, and occasionally exhibit violence.

The violent offenders, especially sex offenders and murderers, attempt escapes less frequently, begin their criminal careers later, fail to respond to community intervention, have family problems that are rarely detected, and often continue their violent criminal career.

Corrections professionals must recognize that the programs and resources directed to either property or violent offenders must be specifically tailored for each group. Neither can be ignored.

Jeanne C. Cyriaque is director of research and systems development for the Harris County, Texas, Juvenile Probation Department, Houston, Texas.

Tracking Children Within a Regional Delinquency Prevention System

Richard S. Everitt

Critical information can be immediately available to professionals, but cooperation among agencies, services, and professionals is essential.

W hen working with troubled children who are at the greatest risk of penetrating the traditional juvenile correctional system, it is necessary to have immediate access to background information to determine adequately their needs. No professional, however qualified or experienced, can make initial decisions without information about the experiences of these children.

This background information should contain statements reflecting educational, psychological, social, and prior delinquent contacts. However, information is traditionally restricted within agencies and departments due to confidentiality laws, rules, or policies. In addition, available information usually takes from two to three days, at best, to get to professional persons eager to make decisions on these cases. Through development of a regional network of child care agencies and use of a shared computer storage base, critical information can be immediately available to professionals, but cooperation among agencies, services, and professionals is essential.

Southeast Alabama Youth Services began through the efforts of several individuals, groups, and agencies in Dothan, Alabama, in 1971, when a citizen rallied support for a specialized counseling program in response to the drug-related murder of a Dothan youth. Drug-related problems became the springboard from which the comprehensive family counseling program would develop.

This program began with a hot line of local volunteers providing information to youths with drug-related problems and their parents.

With an increasing awareness that youths had additional needs, by January 1973, a committee of community leaders was successful in acquiring the services of a full-time youth counselor to plan, coordinate, and establish a youth service program.

The youth counselor and youth committee worked hard to organize a force of professionals to work with youths and tie existing fragmented programs together. From this effort, the Southeast Alabama Youth Service, Inc., evolved in April 1973. It is a nonprofit organization capable of coordinating efforts of law enforcement, juvenile courts, and public welfare agencies and advocating the development of youth service programs for southeast Alabama.

Southeast Alabama Youth Services had a strong voice in developing a State Department of Youth Services in 1974, an agency with statewide responsibility for delinquent youths and youths in need of supervision. The two organizations worked closely together in developing local juvenile delinquency prevention programs. Southeast Alabama Youth Services successfully established a network of counselors available to work on a 24-hour basis with neglected youths or youths with minor problems in southeast Alabama. At the same time, the Department of Youth Services established a program of juvenile counselor/probation officers through the local courts to handle youths who had violated the law.

By 1978, Southeast Alabama Youth Services developed a residential program for neglected or abused youths. Two group attention homes were started that later also facilitated delinquent youths and youths in need of supervision committed by the state.

The program was further expanded in January 1980, when the Diversion Center—a regional, secure diagnostic and evaluation center—was opened to assess and determine adequate treatment for youths' problems.

Since its inception as a regional, nonprofit, public juvenile delinquency prevention agency in April 1973, Southeast Alabama Youth Services has grown from a one-counselor operation into an eight-county, multiprogram youth service bureau. The agency now has counseling services in all eight counties, two group attention homes, a secure diversion center, and numerous local outreach programs.

Since the residential facilities have been fully operational, they have provided care to more than 4,000 children. Before the Diversion

Center was opened, southeast Alabama had at least 500 children in local jails; today it has none. Before the Diversion Center was opened, southeast Alabama had an average of about 300 children committed each year to state institutions; by 1983, it averaged less than 50 committed, regionwide. These improvements in handling and processing children brought to the Board's attention the need for a method to keep up with client files.

Need for a Microcomputer

In 1980, Southeast Alabama Youth Services was recognized by the Office of Juvenile Justice and Delinquency Prevention as a national model for juvenile delinquency prevention programs and, therefore, needed statistical information about its activities. The State Department of Youth Services needed statistical information on children contacted within the region from Southeast Alabama Youth Services. The Alabama Department of Pensions and Securities needed to be informed on the movement of abused and neglected children in the region. Southeast Alabama, with eight juvenile court judges and 14 juvenile probation officers, needed statistical information on juvenile offenders in the region. The region has more than 100 major schools that must have statistical information on children placed at the Diversion Center. The board of directors required a monthly statistical report on the children the agency served. The need for information on the children that Southeast Alabama Youth Services had in its residential care daily was a constant burden on staff. In addition, Southeast Alabama Youth Services then was working with the Community Research Center in Illinois on a national jail removal study that required constant statistical information on all juvenile justice systems in the region. The need for information was at its highest level since inception of the agency.

At the end of 1980, the employees and the board of directors agreed that without rapid access to information, it would be impossible to keep pace with information requests of the future. The decision was made to coordinate agency efforts with other state agencies with computers and use this information to establish the best approach for obtaining equipment and programs to automate the filing system. At the time, there were no computers being used for children's records in Alabama in the manner desired.

The agency's first priority was to develop a master file to store all the information staff would need on children coming in contact with the agency. This proved to be one of the biggest tasks. Not only did the computer have to be programmed, but staff had to project what they would need to retrieve from it. After months of planning and discussion, the basic format for input was chosen. Staff decided to use the agency's computer for statistical reporting, intake screening information, statistical research, and regional resource files.

Because Southeast Alabama Youth Services served eight juvenile court jurisdictions, it was imperative a comprehensive manual intake form be designed. Space was designated for a one-page, 90-item intake form that would record information on reason for referral or offense, social information and background, and legal information needed to track the child throughout the region's juvenile justice system. Because of the geographical location of the Diversion Center and need to have a centralized storage resource file, the computer was set up at the Diversion Center. The Diversion Center became the focal point for almost all intake information concerning Southeast Alabama Youth Services' cases. The cooperation between the eight southeast Alabama counties, Southeast Alabama Youth Services, and the State Department of Youth Services had been clearly established, and all parties were eager to cooperate on the project.

Before the computer was obtained, methods of collecting this information manually had been fragmented and incomplete. Staff now had an excellent opportunity to centralize information on all regional intakes within the agency, as well as those using its facilities and resources. Staff began educating counselors, probation officers, court intake officers, youth services residential workers, and all regional professionals who worked with children in trouble. Because staff had designed the intake forms in quadruplicate, it was a simple matter of filling in these forms at intake, mailing one copy to the Diversion Center, and placing the other copies in county offices. Also, counselors and probation officers had additional copies for parents or law enforcement personnel.

Because the intake forms arriving at the Diversion Center were entered into the computer on a daily basis, staff could build a computer storage base daily on all children having contact with any area of the juvenile court system within the region. In 1983, Southeast Alabama Youth Services had a storage base of more than 5,000 files. The agency averaged approximately 230 files per month, or about eight files per day. The information on these residential files was used at the Diversion Center to provide daily house planning.

Statistical Reporting

One of the most time-consuming functions of any regional operation is completing statistical reports. For licensing purposes, the agency is required to provide four monthly statistical reports to the State Department of Youth Services. These reports must be completed for the Boys' Attention Home, the Girls' Attention Home, the Diversion Center, and counselors' activities. Also, each separate juvenile court jurisdiction must complete a monthly statistical report to the State Department of Youth Services on its activities. Using manual files, these reports took weeks to complete. However, with computer files staff can now produce them in a few hours.

The agency is required by its board of directors to provide a monthly statistical report for each board meeting. Again, with the files on the computer these reports are easily produced. The Diversion Center staff also must produce a monthly school activities report. Because the agency may care for a child from one of more than 100 schools in the region, from one to 30 days per month, this report would be almost impossible without a computer. Schools reimburse the Diversion Center for educational services on a daily basis, and they expect this information to be accurate and easily accessible.

The agency receives a monthly reimbursement from the Alabama Food Nutrition Program. The staff also must provide this program with daily population information pertaining to all its residential children. Before the agency had a centralized storage base, this report often would take the combined efforts of six full-time employees more than three days to complete. Now staff can compile it in less than 30 minutes.

With the development of automated files and centralized information, statistical reports that once took weeks to complete now can take less than one day. Hundreds of hours have been saved, allowing employees to direct their time more appropriately to meeting the children's needs.

Probably the single most important function of the computer is providing immediate, factual information to intake staff about children at a crisis point. No child being considered for secure detention can be expected to provide the intake officer all the pertinent information pertaining to his/her case at the initial interview. The first step of the intake procedure at the Diversion Center is to run a computer check on the child. If the child ever had any contact, for any reason, with any component of the youth services system in southeast Alabama, that information is immediately available to intake staff.

Contrary to the belief that information on youths' past records are always a negative influence on detention decisions, staff regularly finds children who might have been detained are released instead to counselors or probation officers having personal knowledge of their cases. Children neglected or abused in the past no longer need to be released to the individuals abusing them. This information can always be stored in the child's file for future use.

On the other hand, staff finds many cases of youths who might have been released had information not been available alerting them to a major problem. Southeast Alabama Youth Services finds it can ensure the same—if not better—degree of confidentiality when files are computerized than when files are manually exchanged between agencies. Naturally, staff cannot expect to store all information on all children in southeast Alabama in the computer, but they can store essential information to alert counselors or probation officers working with these cases.

Statistical Research

Research and evaluation are very important aspects of program design and development. An agency wants to know why a particular child was brought in, why the child should be detained, if the staff is using the same decision criteria every time, whether the intake staff has considered every other possible resource before detention, and why and how these decisions are made. Without a computer it would be difficult to collect this information and impossible to coordinate it. Because of the ability to do such a detailed study, Southeast Alabama Youth Services is finding factual information on its needs and performances it previously only suspected. With this knowledge, the agency is better prepared to support its existing successful programs and make necessary adjustments where needed.

Due to sheer numbers of professional personnel, agencies, and jurisdictions within the eight rural counties in southeast Alabama, it has become physically impossible to provide all of them with the necessary information without an automated data filing system. Each separate county juvenile court system has statistical requests pertaining to types of cases by workers, cities, race, sex, etc. Without a computer base, staff would constantly be researching the agency's manual files to provide this information.

Staff have found that children who have run away, are missing for some reason or have valid juvenile pick-up orders may never be located without a centralized computer base file to which law enforcement officers may refer on a regular basis. These files are updated regularly and provide local law enforcement personnel with valuable timesaving information. The Diversion Center has files that provide the agency with daily information enabling staff to track youths in its custody from anywhere in the region on immediate demand. The computer at the Diversion Center is operational seven days per week, 24 hours per day and has never requested a coffee break since going on-line.

A New World

As Southeast Alabama Youth Services continues to grow, it appears the computer system will have to grow to keep pace with the agency's increasing need for information. The agency has added additional equipment to its inventory, enabling it to computerize the agency's financial records. Staff now runs all payroll and purchases on computer. Staff also provides information on weekly budget comparisons, purchase order registers, and outstanding obligations categories to monitor the expenditures of all its residential programs and those of its branch counseling offices.

With this additional computer, staff was able to centralize all its financial records in one office and, as a result, maintain more accurate records and controls of overall agency expenditures. The staff reduced its need for support personnel and reduced its overall personnel budget. The agency now has a computerized inventory of equipment. With the inventory program, staff can track equipment purchases and their locations within the agency. As equipment is replaced, staff can maintain a record of how and where it was dispersed.

Southeast Alabama Youth Services has discovered computers can be used effectively within its agency. With a minimal amount of professional personnel, it can design programs for its specific needs. Computers have opened up a new world of information to the agency staff and board of directors. The staff feels that it now has the capability of tracking a youth from his/her first contact and providing assistance as the youth matures through the best possible, positive intervention.

Richard S. Everitt is an educational consultant for Pan Handle Area Educational Cooperative, Chipley, Florida.

Turnstile Children:
Falling Between the Cracks

Eliot Hartstone, Ph.D.

What qualifies a youth as 'mentally disordered' and a 'juvenile offender' must be clearly articulated and should reflect state priorities.

A continuing critical problem confronting juvenile justice practitioners and policymakers is the care and treatment of mentally disordered juvenile offenders. State and local attempts to establish an effective delivery system for providing mental health services to juvenile offenders have been frustrated constantly by lack of information available to resolve the associated programmatic and structural issues. For judges, agency administrators, program planners, and legislators to make knowledgeable decisions regarding dispositions, legislation, and treatment of this hard-to-treat population, much information is needed and fundamental questions must be addressed and answered.

The first step is defining exactly the type of youths to be targeted and how they will be identified. What qualifies a youth as "mentally disordered" and a "juvenile offender" must be clearly articulated and should reflect state priorities. The following concerns should be addressed in defining the target population.

- *Mentally Disordered:* How severe an emotional or mental health problem must the youth possess to be considered for special attention? Must the youth be psychotic? Must he/she have a *DSM-III* diagnosis? Can he/she have a serious emotional disorder? The severity level necessary for the problem to merit attention must be determined and the criteria worded clearly.

- *Juvenile Offender:* Does the state want to target all juvenile offenders with a "mental health" problem, or will the state focus its special attention on only a certain type of juvenile offender (e.g., violent, serious, repeat)? If it limits its focus to certain categories of juvenile offenders, what legal processing is required for qualification (apprehension, filing a petition, court adjudication)?

To develop and implement a special program for "mentally disordered juvenile offenders," such definitions, criteria, and processes are required and need to be articulated. Issues of fairness, equal protection, and labeling are involved. In areas as ambiguous as mental health diagnosis, reliability is an issue; it is not unlikely that different professionals will define individual clients differently. The designation of an ultimate authority to say when a youth satisfies program criteria must be determined carefully.

Before developing the approach for responding to the targeted population, it is important the state acquire an empirical data base on the scope of the problem. Clearly, one of the variables that affects determining the preferred approach is the number to be served.

Currently, there is no national data base on the scope of the problem (Knitzer 1982; Bederow and Reamer 1981). However, there have been several state studies that attempted to determine the extent of the problem in their respective juvenile justice systems (e.g., Massachusetts, Michigan, New Mexico, and New York). While all the studies documented a sizeable population needing services, research conducted through these state efforts varied considerably in the criteria used for inclusion (Cocozza 1982; Commonwealth of Massachusetts 1977; Michigan Departments of Management and Budget, Mental Health, and Social Services 1982; New Mexico Statewide Task Force on Secure Treatment for Violent, Mentally Ill Youth 1982). Further, perhaps reflecting differences in criteria and identification processes, the state studies produced considerable variation in the number of youths defined as requiring special services.

Thus, information currently available is not sufficient to allow program development decisions without conducting local assessments of youths to determine the number of mentally disordered juvenile offenders needing care and treatment. This assessment is an essential preliminary step to rational program development.

Agency Responsibility

Perhaps the most controversial issue in developing programs for this population is determining the agency or agencies responsible for providing care and treatment. In some states, policy for adjudicated delinquents is retention by and treatment within the juvenile corrections department (e.g., the Colorado Division of Youth Services' Closed Adolescent Treatment Center; the Arizona Department of Corrections' Alamo Program). The position taken in such states is that youths adjudicated delinquent and committed to the state's corrections authority are the responsibility of that agency, and that agency should have necessary resources, manpower, and programs to respond to various types of juvenile offenders.

In other states the opinion is youths are more appropriately served under the auspices of state mental health agencies due to their experience and expertise in treating mentally disordered individuals. In some instances such programs are operated by the state mental health department (e.g., Oregon's Child and Adolescent Secure Treatment Program); in other states they are contracted to private providers and monitored by the state mental health department (e.g., the Massachusetts Regional Adolescent Program). Youths in these programs generally are removed from the jurisdiction of the state juvenile corrections agency.

Still other state programs have been developed reflecting the philosophy that the needs of these youths do not fit neatly into any one department, but rather cut across departmental responsibilities and capabilities, bringing about the interagency approach. Some state programs have taken the form of interagency facilities operated for some subset of mentally disordered juvenile offenders (e.g., the Bronx Court-Related Unit for violent offenders; the Illinois Tri-Agency Program for serious offenders).

There appears to be no consensus of opinion about appropriate responsibilities and roles for various state agencies and departments concerning the mentally disordered juvenile offender. There may be isolated instances of both types of agencies claiming responsibility for these youths. Budgetary incentives for administrators are not insignificant, but these incentives may not be equally perceived by line staff in either corrections or mental health facilities. In reality, the typical scenario is that nobody wants these youngsters (Bederow and Reamer 1981). Each department typically tries to place these youths into another department. The result is these youngsters are bounced back and forth; they become known as "turnstile children" who "fall between the cracks" (Bederow and Reamer 1981).

Unless responsibility is formally assigned to one or both of these agencies, it is likely state juvenile corrections and mental health agencies will have little incentive to provide appropriate services. This is especially true as juvenile corrections facilities continue to experience overcrowding and a "hardening" of their residents' profiles. Unfortunately, no data base is available to determine which agency approach is most successful in developing appropriate treatment services.

A fourth crucial issue concerns whether services for the population should be provided directly by the state or through a contract with a private provider. The role that private nonprofit (and for-profit) organizations increasingly play in caring for adult and juvenile offenders renders this question particularly important. Whether advantages of contracting such services outweigh disadvantages appears to vary from one location to another, depending on such issues as:

- Availability of experienced, reputable, and high-quality private providers
- State's capacity to monitor services provided by private vendors
- State budget allocated for treating this population
- Existence of appropriate public facilities for servicing these youths
- Number of juvenile offenders in the state suffering mental disorders and, therefore, the cost effectiveness of maintaining special state facilities, programs, and staff

States electing to use a private contractor network should encourage a diversity of settings and modalities to provide opportunities for settings tailored to individual needs for security and treatment. Institutional approaches should include staff training and skills development for the unique treatment needs of this population.

Special Facilities

Another important, difficult decision concerns whether the need exists to develop special facilities. This problem must be addressed regardless of how a state resolves the issue of primary agency responsibility.

It appears the option adopted most frequently is to maintain these youths in general inmate population, then request appropriate facility staff to provide the youths with "enriched" mental health services as needed. To this end, most corrections facilities hire some clinical staff members (e.g., psychiatric social worker, psychologist). While this appears to be the most frequent approach taken, it also seems to be the one that most often promotes underidentification of disturbed youngsters and underutilization of mental health treatment. By keeping mentally disordered youths in general inmate population, they become the responsibility of line staff not trained to notice and respond to mental health problems. Further, special mental health staff usually are hired at a very high resident-to-staff ratio. Juvenile corrections staff have suggested that when corrections agencies face budget cuts, clinical staff are eliminated first because they are viewed as a luxury rather than a necessity. Youths suffering from serious mental health problems who are cared for in the general population are at risk of not receiving necessary services and treatment. For these reasons, the most frequently used approach, while probably the least expensive, also appears to invite the most difficulties.

Most states directing special attention to this population have done so by developing a special secure facility to respond to the serious juvenile offender suffering from a mental disorder (e.g., New York Bronx Court-Related Unit, California's Wintu Lodge, the Intensive Reintegration Unit in Illinois, the Closed Adolescent Treatment Center in Colorado, or the Alamo Correctional Center in Arizona).

Some special units or programs seem warranted and useful. But states forced to rely solely on such facilities may ignore a sizeable percentage of youths in the delinquent population needing mental health intervention. Not all juvenile offenders requiring mental health services need secure care or have committed serious offenses. There is a wide variety of offenders requiring assistance. Such an approach, taken by itself, ignores the fact that juvenile offenders change with respect to their security needs and, as such, should move progressively through different types of facility care into the community. A one-facility approach does not allow for either placing different types of mentally disordered juveniles into different types of facilities or moving a youth gradually into the community through different security levels. Community reintegration suffers, as youths are unprepared for the contingencies and demands of daily neighborhood life.

Innovations

An alternative to using one special facility for mentally disordered juvenile offenders is developing a comprehensive program that affects the treatment youths receive in many facilities. At least two approaches currently are being tried that address the problem of having a continuum of care available to this population. One is in New York, the other in North Carolina.

New York's Mobile Mental Health Teams: Based on a New York State Office of Mental Health (OMH) study conducted in 1978, it was determined that at least 335 youths in the New York State Division for Youth (DFY) needed specialized mental health care. Subsequently, DFY requested help from OMH in working with these and other youths. In June 1979, DFY and OMH developed and implemented Mobile Mental Health Teams (MMHTs) to respond to the needs of DFY youths through the state.

The MMHTs serve at the various types of DFY facilities and programs throughout the state (e.g., training schools, residential centers, and short-term residential centers). Four mobile mental health teams were developed to serve each of the six clusters of DFY facilities, with each team consisting of a psychologist, psychiatric social worker, and additional staff as determined regionally (e.g., nurses). Each team is affiliated with and accountable to an OMH children's psychiatric center. Each team goes to DFY facilities four days a week to assist DFY facilities and programs. One day a week the team goes to the children's psychiatric center for purposes of supervision, training, and dealing with clinical issues. The range of services provided by the MMHTs for DFY include:

- Assessment of youths in care to determine those needing mental health interventions (i.e., diagnostic evaluations)
- Assistance to DFY staff in developing treatment plans for identified youths
- Implementation and follow-up of treatment plans (i.e., coordinating services, individual counseling and group therapy, acting as advocate for youths in an OMH system, monitoring progress of youths in the OMH children's psychiatric center)
- Assistance to DFY staff in resolution of crisis situations
- Training of DFY staff in treatment and management of youths with emotional disturbances and behavior disorders

Thus, this approach uses a specially developed state mental health department program (e.g., MMHT) to assist the juvenile corrections department in providing mental health interventions to youths within the DFY who have mental health problems.

North Carolina's "Willie M." Program: In response to a 1979 class action lawsuit filed in federal district court against the governor, North Carolina developed and implemented a comprehensive state system to provide services to all minors who "now or in the future suffer from serious emotional, mental, or neurological handicaps accompanied by violent or assaultive behavior..." (Guthrie and Finger 1983). As a result of an out-of-court settlement, the state of North Carolina agreed to provide each child under 18 in the class "placement and services as are actually needed as determined by an individualized habitualization plan rather than such placements and services as are currently available" (Guthrie and Finger 1983).

The following are some of the key components of the system developed in North Carolina:

- Case Management—Case managers, with a 12- to 15-youth caseload, oversee development and execution of an individualized treatment program. Case managers pool together community services and advocate that these youths receive necessary services.
- Five Levels of Treatment—Treatment levels range from highly restricted, locked facilities to day treatment programs. Youths move through levels depending on their rate of progress.
- Behavior Modification—Throughout their treatment in the program, youths earn points that translate into rewards.

- A mix of state and private programs and facilities are used, some of which are solely for youths in projects and others that contain both project and other youths.

It should be noted that the North Carolina "Willie M." program (named after the first plaintiff in the class action) is not restricted to court adjudicated in-state committed youths. Rather, a youth can be defined as assaultive or violent due to behavior documented in his/her case folder, but that may not result in formal court action.

The New York and North Carolina programs demonstrate the capacity to develop and implement innovative, comprehensive programs addressing the special needs of all mentally disordered juvenile offenders. These two programs enable this population to receive care and treatment in the most appropriate and least restrictive placement, and circumvent treatment limitations traditionally present in correctional institutions. Though substantially different in program design, both approaches are characterized by commitment of their agencies to innovation, experimentation, and flexibility in resource strategy. In particular, allocation of scarce service dollars across jurisdictions reflects such agency commitment.

Development of programs for mentally disordered juvenile offenders is not an easy task. Only 11 states have special programs for mentally disordered juvenile offenders (Kerr 1984). Before developing a response to this population, thorough consideration of the key issues mentioned must be undertaken. For each of these issues, information must be gathered, decisions reached, and criteria clearly defined for a state to improve its approach to this population.

Based on the information collected and the decisions made regarding these key issues, a state should be able to initiate developmental work to organize and provide services to a group of youngsters who before were denied access to needed treatment.

REFERENCES

Bederow, Lauri S., and Frederic G. Reamer. 1981. *Treating the Severely Disturbed Juvenile Offender: A Review of Issues and Programs.* Report submitted to the Office of Juvenile Justice and Delinquency Prevention (Grant 79-JN-AX-0018).

Cocozza, Joseph J. 1982. *Characteristics of Children in Out of Home Care.* Albany, N.Y.: New York State Council of Children and Families.

Commonwealth of Massachusetts. 1977. *The Issue of Security in a Community Based System of Juvenile Corrections.* L. Scott Harshbarger, Chairman. Boston, Mass.: Massachusetts Department of Youth Services.

Guthrie, Kendall, and Bill Finger. 1983. " 'Willie M.' Treatment for Disturbed Youngsters," *North Carolina Insight,* Vol. 6, No. 2-3.

Kerr, Charlotte. 1982. "Facilities for the Mentally Ill Juvenile Offender," Paper presented at the 1982 Annual Meeting of the American Society of Criminology, Toronto, Canada.

Knitzer, J. 1982. *Unclaimed Children: The Failure of Public Responsibility to Children and Adolescents in Need of Mental Health Services.* Washington, D.C.: Children's Defense Fund.

Michigan Departments of Management and Budget, Mental Health and Social Services. *Report of the Task Force on the Mentally Ill Adolescent Offender.* Chairpersons: Charles R. Devoli and Hanley Stock. Lansing, Mich.: Michigan Office of Criminal Justice.

New Mexico Statewide Task Force on Secure Treatment for Violent, Mentally Ill Youth. 1982. *Final Report.* Chairpersons: Irving N. Berlin and Phillip J. Wist. Albuquerque, N.M.

Eliot Hartstone, Ph.D., is program manager of juvenile and criminal justice with the URSA Institute, San Francisco, California.

Working With Troubled Youths: Considerations for the New Professional

Daniel J. Maloney

Enthusiasm is certainly an asset that can be used constructively; however, it can be a potential liability. The overzealous new worker can make mistakes that later create serious obstacles.

As an individual begins a profession, there are many new things to learn. A majority of these new skills and knowledge can be learned only in the work setting. Reading and course work help prepare an individual for his/her field; however, much more is learned through practical experience. This is particularly true for the new teacher, counselor, or family worker dealing with troubled youths.

During the first weeks and months of a person's career, it is crucial to establish an effective approach for working with young people. There are many considerations, conflicts, and issues that can be anticipated beforehand and be of valuable assistance to the new professional.

Completing formal education and beginning a new career is tremendously exciting. The opportunity is now at hand to "set the world on fire!" Enthusiasm is certainly an asset that can be used constructively in working with troubled youths; however, it can be a potential liability. The overzealous, new worker can make mistakes that later create serious obstacles.

Good advice to the new professional dealing with troubled young people is start out slowly. Enthusiasm can cause blindness. Harness enthusiasm until greater confidence is gained. Once you have a thorough understanding of your work, then let the enthusiasm go!

Establish a relationship with a co-worker who can serve as a mentor during the initial stages of work adjustment. Also, observe how other staff members function. Take note of the varying relationships they establish with young people.

Be yourself. Develop your own style, making the most of your personality and abilities, but know your limitations. Attempts to copy another staff member's style will be transparent. Blend new skills with your true personality to become an effective worker. Young people will test you. Do not be afraid to admit you are unsure of a procedure or do not know the answer to a question. More respect will be gained by dealing with such situations realistically and honestly.

Talk to co-workers to find out how they approach their work; discuss things they find most difficult and how they handled their initial adjustment. Recognize that some co-workers might not be as enthusiastic as you. Do not adopt a cynical attitude just to be accepted. This will ultimately cause you to be less effective in your work.

It is difficult to help troubled young people and deal with your frustrations at the same time. Be in touch with your feelings and do not be afraid to express them. Frustrations and fears will lessen with time. Be patient with yourself. Take time to put things in perspective.

Working with troubled youths is always a team effort. While it is particularly important to obtain the assistance of co-workers in the initial stages, it is also important to recognize that even with experience, consistent cooperation with co-workers will provide the most effective treatment.

An effective team member should communicate observations, conversations, and incidents concerning a given youth that will help others effectively work with the individual. Even the most insignificant information can be important to future situations. Do not fall into the trap of believing you are the only one who can reach a young person, or that you are the only one who cares. These beliefs can distort your role and disrupt effective treatment. Do not interpret failure to reach a youth as a personal failure. This will diminish energy and enthusiasm needed to work with others. These youths have serious problems that usually do not stem from the influence of just one person. Likewise, it can require the work of many individuals to make a change.

Establishing a Relationship

Research regarding work with troubled young people often draws attention to the necessity for establishing a relationship of trust and concern. This relationship can represent the most therapeutic factor. More accurately, a series of relationships with caring and concerned people can begin to make a difference in a troubled youth's life. These relationships are not simply friendships; they must facilitate the youth's growth and change. Such relationships must include expectations, limits, and discipline conveyed with a sense of caring.

When developing a relationship with a troubled young person, it is not uncommon for new professionals to find themselves feeling sorry for troubled youths. Staff members reluctant to make demands on young people because "they have suffered too much already" do youths a disservice by failing to encourage change.

It is important to challenge young people to strive beyond what they feel they are capable of doing. Assist them whenever possible, not by doing for them, but by helping them do for themselves. Small signs of progress should be noted. Let young people know when they are making gains; do not wait for a major breakthrough. Watch for the series of small gains; they are much more significant.

Do not be afraid to get close to youths with whom you work. This can be the secret of success. Yet, do not allow a close relationship to interfere with the ability to be objective. Be consistent and reliable. The lives of these young people have generally been characterized by a lack of stable relationships.

Allow sufficient freedom to move forward and be sure gains in the relationship are made for the youth and not for you. Be aware of your role in the relationship and maintain communication with co-workers to keep this role in perspective.

The challenges of being a human services professional can be overwhelming. It is essential for that professional never to lose sight of his/her human nature. Even the best professionals are not superhuman. Each individual offers a unique life history, particular sensitivities, vulnerabilities, moods, and personality. In working with young people, various feelings are brought forth that actually stem from life experiences. It is necessary to keep some of these feelings in perspective.

Professionals Are Human

Be aware that youths who have been hurt in their own lives will seek to hurt others around them. Troubled young people have an uncanny ability to take note of adult idiosyncrasies and weaknesses. Observing weakness makes these youths feel secure in knowing they have a potentially useful arsenal to use. Realize that insensitive remarks that may be made about you are the result of similar treatment by other adults in the past. Do not fall apart or retaliate. Retaliation only serves to hurt the youth's already poor self-image. Realize that some remarks might just hit home. Deal with feelings by communicating with other staff members.

Recognize your own limitations. Respect yourself when you find you do not have the energy to deal effectively with a certain youth at a given time. Go a bit more slowly when you feel tired or sick. Accept mistakes as part of the human condition. Mistakes can serve as learning experiences. Life will still continue despite them. Maintain your sense of humor. Some things young people do are really funny. Many are just part of the normal development process.

These considerations should help individuals new to human services professions make a smoother adjustment and allow for positive, fulfilling human and professional experiences through the years to follow.

Daniel J. Maloney is executive assistant to the president of Saint Mary's College, Winona, Minnesota.

Handling Violent Juvenile

Edward M. Murphy, Ph.D.

*Frustrated law enforcement officials and an
enraged public are likely to demand that
violent juveniles be waived to adult
jurisdiction and sentenced to long terms of
prison confinement.*

The small number of offenders who commit serious crimes of violence present the most severe test of the juvenile justice system. Successes the system may experience with many are overshadowed by banner headlines reporting the spectacular failures of the violent few. Frustrated law enforcement officials and an enraged public believing the juvenile system cannot reform such serious offenders are likely to demand that violent juveniles be waived to adult jurisdiction and sentenced to long terms of prison confinement.

Juvenile court judges and juvenile corrections officials share this general frustration, but many continue to believe the juvenile system, when well-managed and adequately resourced, can deal effectively with all but a fraction of the most egregious delinquents. Too often, however, programs and resources needed to do the job are unavailable, and juvenile justice professionals are left wondering how successful they could be if only they had full opportunity to give the effort their best shot.

A unique chance to resolve this question arose in 1981, when the Justice Department's Office of Juvenile Justice and Delinquency Prevention (OJJDP) announced its violent juvenile offender research and development initiative. The purpose of the initiative was to conduct comprehensive programs aimed at gradual reintegration of violent offenders from secure facilities into their home communities. At the same time, funds were provided for a systematic research and evaluation effort to test whether well-resourced treatment programs would have the impact predicted by juvenile justice professionals.

After a national competition, five demonstration sites were selected. One of them was Boston, where the Massachusetts Department of Youth Services (DYS) was awarded a contract to implement what became known as the Boston Offender Project. Because DYS runs a largely deinstitutionalized juvenile corrections system, the Boston site offered unusual opportunities and challenges for dealing with violent juveniles. The goal of the Boston Offender Project is to reduce recidivism among violent juveniles, enhance public protection by increasing accountability for major violators, and improve the likelihood of successful reintegration by focusing on the offenders' academic and vocational skills.

Each year approximately 30 juveniles from the Boston area are committed to DYS for offenses that have caused serious bodily harm to victims. Since 1981, half of these offenders have been randomly selected for participation in the Boston Offender Project. The remaining half formed a control group and received the DYS's normal course of secure treatment and aftercare programming. The project sought to improve the typical handling of a violent case in the following ways:

- Developing three coordinated phases of treatment that include initial placement in a small, locked, secure-treatment program; followed by planned transition into a halfway house; and finally, a gradual return to the juvenile's home community
- Assuring delivery of comprehensive services by assigning experienced caseworkers responsible for working intensively with a case load of not more than eight violent offenders and their families
- Providing services focused on increasing the educational level of offenders and tying educational programs to the marketplace, significantly increasing the prospects of meaningful employment

Elizabeth Pattullo, director of DYS's Metropolitan Region and the project's administrator, says the key to this approach is "intensive involvement of a single caseworker who is responsible for a case load of not more than eight violent offenders from the time of their commitment until they are finally discharged." Caseworkers working with offenders who are not part of the project carry as many as 25 cases and, of necessity, have less contact with each youngster, particularly the small number in locked settings. In contrast, project caseworkers make two visits each week to the Westborough Secure

Treatment Program, the 15-bed facility designated to handle the locked portion of the project.

Treatment Phases

Caseworkers and facility staff conduct comprehensive diagnostic evaluations, educational testing, and medical screening during the initial phase when the offender is in secure detention. The perspective of the courts, police, victims, and community are brought to bear. Assessment results then are incorporated into a treatment plan. Project caseworkers play an important role during this preliminary phase by providing intensive counseling, supporting family involvement, and developing recreational activities. The average length of stay in secure care is approximately eight and a half months.

The second phase, placement in a structured community-based group home, takes place at two primary sites. Ambrose House in Boston and Hastings House in Cambridge are private programs run under contract by Massachusetts Half-way Houses, Inc. This non-profit organization has extensive experience treating adult and juvenile offenders using a successful no-nonsense approach. The group homes afford the opportunity for offenders to test gains made in the secure phase in an open setting as an interim step in returning home. Job placement, admission to a school program, and development of a relationship with group home staff are usually accomplished before the youth is transferred from Westborough.

On completion of the second phase, most project participants return home to live with families. Caseworkers deliberately increase involvement with youths and families during this phase to ensure smooth reintegration into the community. Good behavior is rewarded with faster movement through the phases; poor behavior is discouraged through a parole revocation process that includes the possibility of returning to the Westborough Secure Treatment Unit. Having the capacity to move youths quickly up or down within the system and placing primary responsibility for that decision on the case manager is an important element of the project.

Throughout the entire treatment process, consistent emphasis is placed on project involvement with the police, courts, probation, and other justice and human service system components. The caseworker works closely with these agencies to keep those concerned informed of the youth's progress and to develop a support system for the violent juvenile offender who successfully completes his/her treatment program.

Effective Response

In examining the experience of project participants when compared to a control sample of offenders handled in the normal way, the following differences emerged:

- All project participants went to a community residential program on release from secure treatment. Only 42 percent of the control group was placed in such a program before returning home.
- Seventy-nine percent of project participants were able to find unsubsidized employment, as compared to 29 percent of the control group.
- Seventy-five percent of project youths continued in an educational program after being released from the secure setting, compared to 46 percent of the control group.
- Finally, only one-third of the experimental group has been rearrested. This represents a substantial decrease from general recidivism rates across the nation and in DYS for similar high-risk offenders.

The Boston Offender Project is not the solution to the problem of serious juvenile crime. The project is, however, an effective response to violent youngsters who come into the juvenile corrections system. In the words of J. Bryan Riley, executive director of Massachusetts Half-way Houses, Inc.: "What we have done with this project is nothing more than all the commonsense things our experience has taught us. But we have gone about it in an organized and disciplined way. We have seen that an energetic juvenile justice system can handle the toughest kids."

Treatment Differences

PROJECT ELEMENTS	CONTROL GROUP	PROJECT GROUP
Diagnostic Assessments	• Standard psychological assessment, updated on an irregular basis.	• Comprehensive, ongoing assessments to measure needs and developments in psychological, vocational, and medical areas.
Caseworkers	• Average experience 12 months in juvenile justice system. • Twenty-five active cases. • Passively involved in treatment programs. Coordinator of services.	• Average experience three years in juvenile justice system. • Seven active cases. • Actively involved in treatment programs. Responsible for delivery of treatment.
Secure Programs	• Caseworker visits one time per month.	• Caseworker visits two times per week.
Non-Secure Residential	• May not be offered as part of a gradual reentry. • Not serving a primarily post-secure treatment population. • Limited flexibility to return to secure care. • Low staff-to-client ratio.	• Automatically the first step in reintegration. • Serving an exclusive violent, secure-treatment population. • Flexibility to move up and down the continuum (including back to secure treatment). • High staff-to-client ratio.
Aftercare	• Moderate involvement by caseworkers. • Irregular contact with families. • Termination at age 18.	• Increasing involvement by caseworkers. • Regular contact with families. • Planned termination before or after age 18, depending on treatment plan.

Edward M. Murphy, Ph.D., is commissioner of the Massachusetts Department of Mental Health, Boston, Massachusetts.

Teen Court: Involving Young People in the Judicial Process

Natalie Rothstein

'In teen court the teens are the authority and the establishment. . . . Teen court places a high priority on educating young people to the responsibilities of being an individual, family member, and citizen.'

Widespread public interest has surrounded the Odessa, Texas, Teen Court due to its uniqueness and the desire of many communities to find an effective way to curb juvenile crime. Until the mid-1970s there were many gaps in the juvenile justice system. Young people apprehended for misdemeanors such as shoplifting or public intoxication merely were given a lecture and sent home. Experts in the field began to realize juvenile crime could be reduced if first offenders were made accountable for their acts by involving them in a positive way with the judicial system before law-breaking behavior became a pattern. This realization lies at the heart of the teen court concept.

Seattle, Washington, and Denver, Colorado, were among the first cities to fund youth diversion and accountability programs. Denver's program funded by the district attorney's office with a budget of $40,000 is a good example. Statistics showed that youths under age 18 were committing 55 percent of all crimes in the city.

The Denver program sought to relieve the juvenile court docket and keep youthful offenders from returning to court. It allowed a juvenile arrested for a misdemeanor—use of marijuana, automobile theft, liquor violation, or shoplifting—to choose between two adjudicatory methods: the traditional court or the newly established diversion program. If diversion were chosen, the offender had to plead guilty and sign a contract to make restitution to the victim or engage in community service. Even parental counseling could be written into the contract. Denver also allowed a student jury to hear cases and mete out punishment. Recidivism among participants was less than 15 percent.

Teenagers in Charge

Odessa has carried Denver's plan a step further by allowing young people to be nearly the complete authority in the court process. Teenagers act as jurors, bailiffs, and attorneys. Only the judge, an unpaid volunteer, is an adult. Moreover, trials in teen court take place in a realistic setting, the district courtroom of the county courthouse.

Funded by the city of Odessa and Odessa's Junior League, the teen court began conducting its first trials in November 1983. The Junior League had spent three years researching juvenile diversion and accountability programs in the hope of reducing Odessa's high juvenile crime rate. The city had a high adult crime rate during this time as well and was labeled the nation's "murder capital."

The court's concept began with the premise that young people, once involved in the judicial process, rarely run afoul of the law again. This concept held true for Odessa. Since the program's inception, more than 760 cases have been heard, with recidivism among participants ranging between 10 and 15 percent for traffic offenses and zero for Class C misdemeanors (attempted criminal trespass, simple assault, shoplifting under $20, and other minor offenses).

The success of the Odessa Teen Court has prompted city council to approve extending the cases to be heard by the court to more serious Class B misdemeanors, including minor drug possession cases. Officials hope this change might do something about the growing drug abuse problem. "Teenagers need to know that their peers do not condone unsafe driving or 'smoking a joint.' It is the peers who start young people into these behaviors and it is the peers who can keep them out of it," one teenage teen court attorney said. Odessa's success also has led to a grant from Texas' Criminal Justice Division enabling the court to hire a certified drug abuse counselor to teach a monthly course for defendants.

Teen court juries comprise teenagers recruited from two local high schools. Defendants may be sentenced to serve on the juries from one to four times, depending on the seriousness of the offense. Jury panels split evenly between former defendants and volunteers are common. Bailiffs, clerks, defense attorneys, and prosecuting attorneys are also teenagers. Only the judge is an adult. After an orientation meeting and briefing by the judge before each week's trials youngsters rarely have to be told what to do. To date, the judge has not altered a single verdict.

The defendants, who range in age from 10 to 16 years old, must plead guilty. They are referred to the teen court by the municipal court judge in cases of traffic citations or by the police department's juvenile detective division in cases of Class C misdemeanors. Youngsters can choose to be tried in municipal court and pay the fine for traffic offenses or plead guilty and be tried by the teen court. If the latter course is chosen, the youngster's record remains unblemished. If a youngster does not like the sentence, he/she can refuse to comply and return to municipal court for disposition of the case. This has happened only once since teen court began operating.

Community Service

Sentences are always for community service (up to 22 hours) and jury service. Community services performed by the young people include working at the animal shelter, library, or nursing homes; picking up trash at the ball fields; and working for the parks department, police department, or any other community agency. Agencies involved are pleased about the program because they obtain free, conscientious labor at a time when budget cutbacks are hampering programs. One interesting side effect is many of these young people return to the agencies as volunteers after their "sentences" have been served.

The program may be beneficial in other ways. Prior to the inception of the Odessa Teen Court, the recidivism rate of all juvenile offenders in Odessa was 50 to 60 percent. Although there is no evidence to suggest that teen court is responsible, one municipal court judge reported fewer teenage traffic violators in court, which he attributed to the presence of the new teen court.

Many of the youngsters appearing before the teen court develop an interest in the legal system. Many return after their jury trials seeking a chance to be lawyers, bailiffs, clerks, or jurors. Between 100 and 150 youths have stayed with the program since its inception. "It is hoped that the Odessa Teen Court will interrupt developing patterns of criminal behavior by promoting feelings of self-esteem, motivation for self-improvement, and development of a healthy attitude toward authority," one judge commented. "In teen court the teens are the authority and the establishment." And, he adds, "Teen court places high priority on educating young people to the responsibilities of being an individual, family member, and citizen."

Natalie Rothstein is coordinator of Teen Court, Odessa Municipal Court, Odessa, Texas.

Probation as Therapy

Joseph F. Sweet

If, for a brief, flickering instant, adolescents in trouble can have an unconditional, respectful, honest relationship—even with a probation counselor—it could give them the courage to find trust again.

Mike cocked back the ashtray as if to throw it at his probation counselor. He was angry and determined not to be pushed around anymore. The probation counselor, he thought, was asking too much of him. Mike felt he could not stay in the vocational program. He just could not make it.

Jack was Mike's probation counselor, and he knew Mike was testing him to see if he was really different from Mike's parents. Mike, age 15, had been on probation for three months. He had marginally diminished learning capacities and a slightly deformed right arm. He had no friends, and because he was on probation for assaulting his mother and sister, his family's support was tenuous. His parents obviously were disappointed and angry about the assault, feelings probably having a long history.

Mike had taken quickly to his probation counselor. He enjoyed the attention and interest the man showed in him. Considering the boy's history, it was inevitable that Mike would maneuver a critical incident to test Jack. Mike was scared of the genuine relationship he was developing with Jack. He had to act. So, he refused to return to school and dared his probation counselor to make him do so, unconsciously measuring Jack's reaction.

Jack knew he had to respond differently than Mike's parents. He could not appear angry or disappointed with Mike's behavior. Jack's task was to break the frustrating cycle of Mike's relationships. His response reflected Mike's feelings: "I know you are angry.... Let's talk about what you are afraid of at school." Yet he maintained the parameters of acceptable behavior: "You cannot intimidate me." By adopting this approach, Jack was able to dispel Mike's anger. They then were able to discuss some of Mike's fears about school. Jack was the first person in Mike's life who did not lay blame.

Jack sparked a feeling in Mike that had lain dormant for years. Mike was accustomed to fighting, but he was not accustomed to someone caring. Jack seemed more interested in helping Mike than in proving what a jerk Mike was. Despite the feeling of mutual warmth, Mike remained guarded and suspicious. Jack knew he had gained a large measure of Mike's trust, but he also knew the testing was not over.

Breaking Patterns

In general, we tend to encourage others to treat us the way we have been treated by our families. We seek the comfortable and the familiar. We know how to act in these situations. Familiar situations tend to reinforce our world view. If we believe people to be generally honest, we encourage that honesty and seek out honest persons for our relationships. By recapitulating our familiar relationships, we discourage ourselves from having to rethink our prejudices and ideas about others.

Juvenile delinquents are particularly susceptible to rigid thought patterns. They typically have dysfunctional primary relationships that encourage similar dysfunctional relationships. The abused girl, for example, often marries a man who abuses her. She, in turn, abuses her own children, thus continuing the cycle.

The juvenile delinquent becomes suspicious of people who act differently from his parents. One intelligent young boy, who fashioned himself a con-man, was convinced everyone was on the "take," and everything had an angle. He searched diligently to find similar behavior in other people and was satisfied when he found it. If he could not find it, he would encourage or even manufacture it. He felt his world view should prevail, despite the facts.

Typical acting-out adolescents attempt to elicit familiar responses from important adults around them: parents, teachers, police, counselors, and others. These youngsters encourage those around them to feel the rejection, anger, and/or distrust that are familiar to them. Although they may approach adults in an extremely pleasing manner, attempting to win their approval and love, these relationships are doomed to failure. This type of adolescent is a product of manipulative relationships. Learning well from their primary relationships, they assume their relationships will be of the same quality. They expect them to be so, unwittingly encouraging this self-defeating process.

When an adolescent is experiencing dysfunctional relationships, the juvenile probation counselor is in a strategic position to break the repetitive chain of such relationships. As a personification of authority, the probation counselor is an ideal target for the teenager's anger. At times, the relationship also can provide a unique opportunity for therapeutic intervention into the youngster's life. In effect, the probation counselor can be the good parent the child never had.

Steps Toward Trust

Probation as therapy can be divided into five distinct steps:

• *Case Review:* The probation counselor needs skills to read the youth's behavior and its probable antecedents. Case record review, family and child interviews, and discussions with other involved professionals are appropriate steps. In particular, the parents' responses to the child should be noted. Is the parent overly angry at the child, or overly protective? Is the child the family scapegoat, or is he/she expected to attain unreachable goals? Insights from a case study can give the probation counselor significant clues as to how the adolescent will expect him/her to react during crises.

• *Self-Awareness:* The probation counselor needs to inspect his/her own reactions to adolescents. Is he/she particularly impatient with "spoiled brats"? Does he/she have a soft spot for blue-eyed, blond-haired waifs? Traditional transference, counter-transference issues must be addressed. Appropriate and involved supervision of a counselor fulfills this need. Without such supervision, the counselor may superimpose his/her own issues on the counselor/client relationship.

• *Developing a Relationship:* Sometimes this takes great patience, but with an understanding of the first two steps the probation counselor will be able to establish a direction. If these children have been rejected, accept them. If they have been put down, build them up. If they lack confidence, let them know you have faith in their ability. Your behavior will intrigue the youngsters. Some may be scared off; all will distrust you. After all, they rarely have been treated with concern and respect before.

• *The Critical Incident:* This is the testing phase of the relationship. In effect, the juvenile delinquent thinks, "Yeah, this is great while I'm doing what he wants, but when I screw up he'll become a jerk just like the rest of them." If a critical incident does not occur naturally, one will be manufactured. It could be truancy, a family fight, criminal involvement, or even rejection of a probation counselor's demands. The adolescent will scrupulously inspect the probation counselor's attitude toward him, comparing it with that of his/her parents.

• *Following Through:* If the probation counselor passes the first critical test, he/she will then encounter more tests. A supportive, structured approach can instill in youngsters good feelings about themselves while helping them understand the demands of the world in a way that will bolster their confidence to meet them. In effect, the probation counselor does some of the parenting the clients' parents failed to do.

This type of action therapy for juveniles is more effective than insight-oriented counseling. Words have been used to deceive delinquent adolescents. They believe actions, not words.

If, for a brief, flickering instant, adolescents in trouble can have an unconditional, respectful, honest relationship—even with a probation counselor—it could be the spark that gives them the courage to find trust again. They may forget you, but they will always remember that feeling.

Joseph F. Sweet is a juvenile probation counselor with the Rhode Island Department for Children and Their Families, Providence, Rhode Island, and also works in a private mental health counseling practice in East Greenwich, Rhode Island.